YORK NOTES

THE TEMPEST

WILLIAM SHAKESPEARE

NOTES BY EMMA PAGE

PEARSON

YORK
PRESS

YORK PRESS
322 Old Brompton Road, London SW5 9JH

PEARSON EDUCATION LIMITED
Edinburgh Gate, Harlow,
Essex CM20 2JE, United Kingdom
Associated companies, branches and representatives throughout the world

First published 2016

10 9 8 7 6 5 4 3 2 1

ISBN 978–1–2921–3814–5

Illustrations by Timo Grubing; and Moreno Chiacchiera (page 53 only)
Phototypeset by Carnegie Book Production
Printed in Slovakia

Photo credits: Vasik Olga/Shutterstock for page 8 / Krasowit/Shutterstock for
page 10 / Anneka/Shutterstock for page 11 / Gordon Saunders/Shutterstock for
page 15 / trekandshoot/Shutterstock for page 17 / S-F/Shutterstock for page 19
/ Kim7/Shutterstock for page 21 / Enlightened'Media/Shutterstock for page 23 /
Mr.Yotsaran/Shutterstock for page 25 / Jagoush/Shutterstock for page 26 / Leicher
Oliver/Shutterstock for page 29 / Anna Morgan/Shutterstock for page 30 / Ron Ellis/
Shutterstock for page 31 / Vlue/Shutterstock for page 32 / Dmitry Skutin/Shutterstock
for page 33 / Galushko Sergey/Shutterstock for page 34 top / worapan kong/
Shutterstock for page 34 bottom / Sergey Nivens/Shutterstock for page 35 / Kostyantyn
Ivanyshen/Shutterstock for page 37 / Inara Prusakova/Shutterstock for page 41 /
PanicAttack/Shutterstock for page 43 / Tatiana Makotra/Shutterstock for page 48
/ Mr Doomits/Shutterstock for page 51 / Artem Musaev/Shutterstock for page 52 /
etabeta1/Alamy for page 54 top / photomaster/Shutterstock for page 54 bottom /
jocic/Shutterstock for page 56 / Jaroslaw Grudzinski/Shutterstock for page 57 / Garsya/
Shutterstock for page 58 top / Annette Shaff/Shutterstock for page 58 bottom / Hulton
Fine Art Collection/Getty for page 59 top / chrisdorney/Shutterstock for page 59
bottom / Tischenko Irina/Shutterstock for page 60 / f9photos/Shutterstock for page 61
/ Isantilli/Shutterstock for page 64 / Andrey Burmakin/Shutterstock for page 65 / Igor
Zh/Shutterstock for page 66 / Valentyn Volkov/Shutterstock for page 67 / apple2499/
Shutterstock for page 68 / wavebreakmedia/Shutterstock for page 77

CONTENTS

PART FOUR:
THEMES, CONTEXTS AND SETTINGS

PART FIVE:
FORM, STRUCTURE AND LANGUAGE

PART SIX:
PROGRESS BOOSTER

PART SEVEN:
FURTHER STUDY AND ANSWERS

PREPARING FOR ASSESSMENT

HOW WILL I BE ASSESSED ON MY WORK ON *THE TEMPEST*?

All exam boards are different, but whichever course you are following, your work will be examined through these four Assessment Objectives:

Assessment Objectives	Wording	Worth thinking about ...
AO1	Read, understand and respond to texts. Students should be able to: ● maintain a critical style and develop an informed personal response ● use textual references, including quotations, to support and illustrate interpretations.	● How well do I know what happens, what people say, do etc.? ● What do *I* think about the key ideas in the play? ● How can I support my viewpoint in a really convincing way? ● What are the best quotations to use and when should I use them?
AO2	Analyse the language, form and structure used by a writer to create meanings and effects, using relevant subject terminology where appropriate.	● What specific things does the writer 'do'? What choices has Shakespeare made (why this particular word, phrase or form here? Why does this event happen at this point?) ● What effects do these choices create? Suspense? Sympathy? Wonder?
AO3	Show understanding of the relationships between texts and the contexts in which they were written.	● What can I learn about society from the play? (What does it tell me about Elizabethan/Jacobean travel and exploration, for example?) ● What was society like in Shakespeare's time? Can I see it reflected in the text of the play?
AO4*	Use a range of vocabulary and sentence structures for clarity, purpose and effect, with accurate spelling and punctuation.	● How accurately and clearly do I write? ● Are there small errors of grammar, spelling and punctuation I can get rid of?

AO4 is not assessed by Edexcel in relation to The Tempest

Look out for the Assessment Objective labels throughout your York Notes Study Guide – these will help to focus your study and revision!

The text used in this Study Guide is the Penguin Shakespeare edition, 2007.

HOW TO USE YOUR YORK NOTES STUDY GUIDE

You are probably wondering what is the best and most efficient way to use your York Notes Study Guide on *The Tempest*. Here are three possibilities:

A step-by-step study and revision guide	A 'dip-in' support when you need it	A revision guide after you have finished the novel
Step 1: Read Part Two as you read the text, as a companion to help you study it. **Step 2:** When you need to, flip forward to Parts Three to Five to focus your learning. **Step 3:** Then, when you have finished, use Parts Six and Seven to hone your exam skills, revise and practise for the exam.	Perhaps you know the play text quite well, but you want to check your understanding and practise your exam skills? Just look for the section you think you need most help with and go for it!	You might want to use the Notes after you have finished your study, using Parts Two to Five to check over what you have learned, and then work through Parts Six and Seven in the immediate weeks leading up to your exam.

HOW WILL THE GUIDE HELP YOU STUDY AND REVISE?

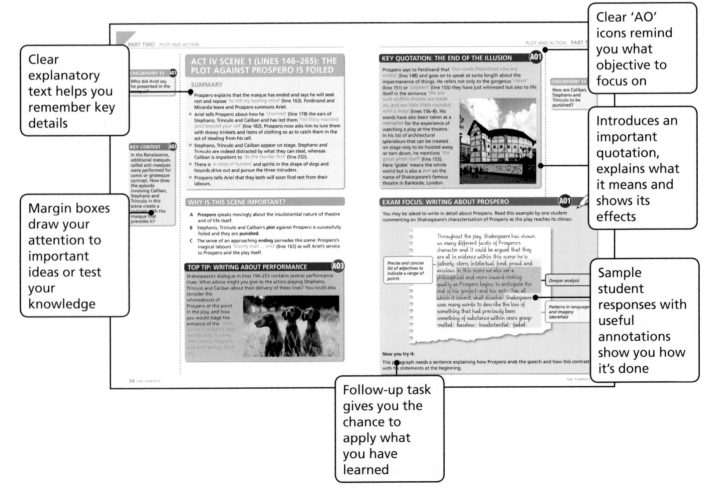

Clear explanatory text helps you remember key details

Margin boxes draw your attention to important ideas or test your knowledge

Clear 'AO' icons remind you what objective to focus on

Introduces an important quotation, explains what it means and shows its effects

Sample student responses with useful annotations show you how it's done

Follow-up task gives you the chance to apply what you have learned

Extra references to help you focus your revision

Themes are explained clearly with bullet points which give you ideas you might use in your essay responses

This section helps you tackle or explore challenging ideas or gives you a deeper insight into the writer's methods

PART FOUR: THEMES, CONTEXTS AND SETTINGS

THEMES

POLITICAL POWER

THEME TRACKER (A01)
Political power
● Act I Scene 2 lines 75–6: Prospero suggests he let his brother become too involved in affairs of state.
● Act II Scene 1 lines 206–8: Antonio urges Sebastian to grasp the opportunity to become king.
● Act V Scene 1: Ferdinand and Miranda's chess game foreshadows their return to Naples as future heads of state.

Many different types of power are at work in *The Tempest*, both human and supernatural. Shakespeare gives us a fascinating insight into the workings of political power in his account of how Prospero lost his dukedom and in his portrayal of the scheming Antonio:

● Prospero explains to Miranda in Act I Scene 2 the circumstances by which he was overthrown as Milan's head of state. He reflects on the factors that led to his downfall, particularly his own fondness for study rather than government and Antonio's 'ambition' (line 105) and 'foul play' (line 62).

● He acknowledges his brother's political skills – 'Being once perfected how to grant suits [favours]/How to deny them, who t'advance, and who/To trash for over-topping' (lines 79–81) – and success in winning the hearts and minds of the people and in 'stooping' (line 116) to the King of Naples to win his favour. He also describes how Antonio's growing ambition made him self-deceiving and increasingly obsessed with power: 'Made such a sinner of his memory/To credit his own lie' (lines 101–2). Antonio's determination to convince Sebastian to oust King Alonso – 'What a sleep were this/For your advancement!' (II.1.267–8) – gives the impression of a man who is greedy for ever more influence.

● Antonio is seen to act unjustly, but he is nonetheless a fascinating portrayal of a cunning and ruthless political operator. We may draw a parallel between his approach to winning and maintaining power with the principles advocated by Niccolò Machiavelli in *The Prince* (1513).

KEY CONTEXT (A03)
In the fourteenth century Italy was comprised of various states of great importance. Milan, Naples, Florence, Venice and the Papal States were all independently ruled.

AIMING HIGH: SHAKESPEARE AND THE CYCLE OF POWER ⭐

The very best answers will show excellent understanding of relevant concepts in their discussion of key themes. For example, political power games, succession and usurpation are ideas Shakespeare returns to again and again in his plays.

Many of Shakespeare's plays depict power struggles and violent usurpations. These include the history plays such as *Richard II* in which the king is overthrown by Henry Bolingbroke and *Henry IV Part 1* in which Bolingbroke (now King Henry) has to defend his crown against a challenger. Shakespeare's most famous tragedies including *Macbeth* and *Hamlet* also show power changing hands by means of treachery and violence. By watching these plays, the audience explores the minds and motivations of rulers and their rivals and witnesses the toppling of powerful figures as time passes and fortune's wheel turns.

54 THE TEMPEST

Parts Two to Five end with a **Progress and Revision Check**:

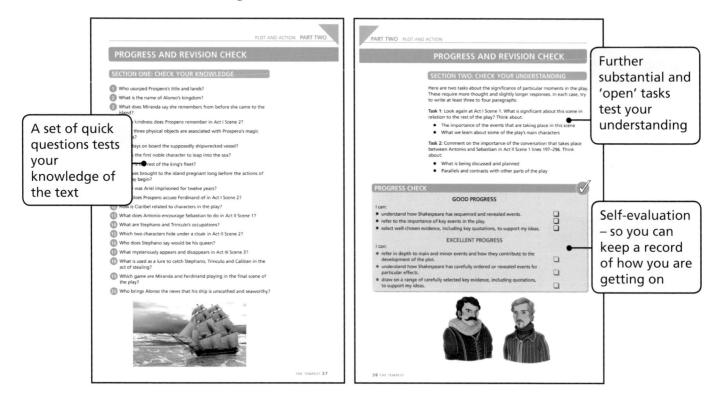

A set of quick questions tests your knowledge of the text

PLOT AND ACTION **PART TWO**

PROGRESS AND REVISION CHECK

SECTION ONE: CHECK YOUR KNOWLEDGE

1. Who usurped Prospero's title and lands?
2. What is the name of Alonso's kingdom?
3. What does Miranda say she remembers from before she came to the island?
4. What kindness does Prospero remember in Act I Scene 2?
5. What three physical objects are associated with Prospero's magic powers?
6. Who stays on board the supposedly shipwrecked vessel?
7. Who is the first noble character to leap into the sea?
8. Where is the rest of the king's fleet?
9. Who was brought to the island pregnant long before the actions of the play begin?
10. Why was Ariel imprisoned for twelve years?
11. Why does Prospero accuse Ferdinand in Act I Scene 2?
12. How is Claribel related to characters in the play?
13. What does Antonio encourage Sebastian to do in Act II Scene 1?
14. What are Stephano and Trinculo's occupations?
15. Which two characters hide under a cloak in Act II Scene 2?
16. Who does Stephano say would be his queen?
17. What mysteriously appears and disappears in Act III Scene 3?
18. What is used as a lure to catch Stephano, Trinculo and Caliban in the act of stealing?
19. Which game are Miranda and Ferdinand playing in the final scene of the play?
20. Who brings Alonso the news that his ship is unscathed and seaworthy?

THE TEMPEST 37

PART TWO PLOT AND ACTION

PROGRESS AND REVISION CHECK

SECTION TWO: CHECK YOUR UNDERSTANDING

Here are two tasks about the significance of particular moments in the play. These require more thought and slightly longer responses. In each case, try to write at least three to four paragraphs.

Task 1: Look again at Act I Scene 1. What is significant about this scene in relation to the rest of the play? Think about:
● The importance of the events that are taking place in this scene
● What we learn about some of the play's main characters

Task 2: Comment on the importance of the conversation that takes place between Antonio and Sebastian in Act II Scene 1 lines 197–296. Think about:
● What is being discussed and planned
● Parallels and contrasts with other parts of the play

PROGRESS CHECK ✓

GOOD PROGRESS
I can:
● understand how Shakespeare has sequenced and revealed events. ☐
● refer to the importance of key events in the play. ☐
● select well-chosen evidence, including key quotations, to support my ideas. ☐

EXCELLENT PROGRESS
I can:
● refer in depth to main and minor events and how they contribute to the development of the plot. ☐
● understand how Shakespeare has carefully ordered or revealed events for particular effects. ☐
● draw on a range of carefully selected key evidence, including quotations, to support my ideas. ☐

38 THE TEMPEST

Further substantial and 'open' tasks test your understanding

Self-evaluation – so you can keep a record of how you are getting on

---

Don't forget **Parts Six** and **Seven**, with advice and practice on **improving your writing skills**:

● Focus on **difficult areas** such as **'context'** and **'inferences'**
● **Short snippets** of **other students' work** to show you how it's done (or not done!)
● Three annotated **sample responses** to a task **at different levels**, with **expert comments**, to help you judge your own level
● **Practice questions**
● **Answers** to the **Progress and Revision Checks** and **Checkpoint** margin boxes

Now it's up to you! Don't forget – there's even more help on our website with more sample answers, essay planners and even online tutorials. Go to www.yorknotes.com to find out more.

PLOT SUMMARY: WHAT HAPPENS IN *THE TEMPEST*?

TOP TIP (A02)

A tempest is a violent storm or commotion. The play's title can be understood on both a literal and symbolic level. Make sure you make notes on both.

ACT I – PROSPERO'S STORM

- King Alonso of Naples's ship is caught in a terrible sea-storm. The boatswain urges his passengers to stay below deck and everyone fears for their lives.

- On an island, Prospero explains to his teenage daughter why they have lived there ever since she can remember. He explains that he used to be the Duke of Milan but his brother Antonio plotted against him.

- We learn that Prospero has magical powers and that his spirit servant Ariel created the storm on Prospero's behalf. Ariel explains that all on board have survived the storm and that Ferdinand has come ashore separately from his father. Ariel yearns to be free, but Prospero reminds him of how he saved him from the witch Sycorax and tells him he has 'more work' (Scene 2 line 238) for him to do.

- Caliban, the son of Sycorax, is the other resident of the island and is Prospero's slave. He curses and complains to Prospero that the island is his by right.

- Ariel's singing leads an enchanted Ferdinand into the presence of Prospero and Miranda. Ferdinand and Miranda are instantly attracted to each other. Prospero accuses Ferdinand of being a 'spy' (Scene 2 line 5) and says he will hold him prisoner.

ACT II – COMING ASHORE

- Gonzalo and Adrian try to comfort an inconsolable Alonso by finding things to praise about the island. We learn that the king was returning from the wedding of his daughter Claribel to the King of Tunis when the storm struck.

- Francisco, a nobleman, says that he saw Ferdinand swim safely to shore but Alonso still fears the worst.

- Gonzalo fantasises about the kind of society he would establish on the island.

- Ariel secretly arrives *'playing solemn music'* and sends everyone but Sebastian and Antonio to sleep. Antonio tells Sebastian how he can win power for himself if he kills his brother Alonso. Sebastian and Antonio are about to make an attempt on the lives of Alonso and Gonzalo when Ariel returns *'with music'* and wakens the sleepers.

- On another part of the island, Caliban complains about Prospero's spirits tormenting him. He hides under a cloak from Trinculo, a jester who has come ashore from the ship. Trinculo says more stormy weather is brewing and shelters under the same cloak.

- Another survivor, a butler called Stephano, arrives and thinks that there must be a strange creature under the cloak. Eventually Stephano and Trinculo recognise each other and swap survival stories. Caliban believes he has found a new and kinder master in Stephano and rejoices.

KEY CONTEXT (A03)

An essay about nature and civilisation by the French writer Michel de Montaigne (1533–92) called 'On Cannibals' is thought to have been a key influence on Shakespeare's play. Gonzalo's rather naive description of his perfect island society in Act II Scene 1 owes a debt to Montaigne's idealised description of the the New World.

ACT III – THE PLAN CONTINUES

- Ferdinand carries wood for Prospero and is inspired in his 'mean task' (Scene 1 line 4) by thinking about his 'mistress' (line 6) Miranda. Miranda arrives, followed by Prospero who is secretly checking on the progress of his plan.

- Ferdinand and Miranda again speak of love and their desire to marry.

- Caliban continues to look up to Stephano and wishes for revenge on Prospero with Stephano's help.

- An invisible Ariel discovers Stephano, Trinculo and Caliban as they drink, quarrel and plot. He enchants them with drumming and leads them away.

- Alonso and the others are tired after searching the island for hours with no sighting of Ferdinand. On behalf of Prospero, Ariel performs an elaborate spectacle for Alonso, Antonio and Sebastian. The three men are accused of overthrowing 'good Prospero' (line 70). The others sleep through the strange vision.

- Prospero praises Ariel's work and says that his enemies are now 'in my power' (line 90).

- Gonzalo is afraid for his 'desperate' (line 104) companions.

ACT IV – A CELEBRATION

- There is a masque to celebrate Miranda and Ferninand's engagement.

- Prospero speaks about how beautiful visions must come to an end and draws a parallel with the end of life. He suddenly remembers he still has business to attend to, since there is still a plot against him.

- Ariel has led the three rogues to a 'filthy-mantled pool' (Scene 1 line 182). Prospero now asks Ariel to catch them with attractive trinkets. Caught in the act of thieving, the intruders are chased off stage.

ACT V AND EPILOGUE– THE END OF THE MAGIC

- Ariel describes to Prospero the 'distracted' (Scene 1 line 12) state of Alonso, Gonzalo and the others. Prospero says he intends to be guided by 'virtue' rather than 'vengeance' (line 28) in dealing with them.

- Prospero renounces magic entirely. Ariel leads the men to Prospero, who speaks to them while they are still in an enchanted state.

- Alonso returns the dukedom to its rightful owner. However Antonio and Sebastian do not ask for Prospero's forgiveness.

- Prospero reveals Ferdinand and Miranda sitting playing chess together. Finally reunited, Ferdinand and Alonso are overjoyed, and Miranda is welcomed into their family.

- The ship's master and boatswain return with news that the ship came through the storm unscathed.

- Prospero's forgiveness is extended to Stephano, Trinculo and Caliban. He invites Alonso and the others to his dwelling before they set sail for Naples and says farewell to Ariel and grants him his freedom.

- Prospero says that his powers are fading. He hopes that the audience has found the performance pleasing and says that its kind words and applause will 'release' (line 9) him.

TOP TIP A01

Consider as you read the play how women are presented by Shakespeare in *The Tempest*. As well as the major character of Miranda, the text also mentions Miranda's mother, Claribel (the King of Naples' daughter) and Sycorax.

KEY CONTEXT A03

In medieval times, earth, air, water and fire were considered essential to all life, and people used them to explain the world and its phenomena. As you read the play, consider the importance of these four elements.

ACT I SCENE 1: A STORM AT SEA

SUMMARY

- A sea-storm is raging and a ship is in trouble.
- The ship's master is concerned the ship could run aground and instructs the boatswain to speak to the ship's mariners.
- The boatswain gives the mariners clear and urgent instructions and insists that King Alonso and the other high-ranking passengers remain in their cabins.
- The king's councillor Gonzalo says that the boatswain should remember 'whom thou hast aboard' (line 19). He is referring to Alonso, King of Naples, to the king's son Ferdinand, and to Antonio, the Duke of Milan. The boatswain says that the 'elements' (line 21) do not respect rank and title.
- Shortly after the courtly characters return to their cabins, the boatswain hears loud cries and howls coming from his passengers. He is exasperated when Sebastian, Antonio and Gonzalo reappear on deck, and the courtiers and boatswain exchange insults.
- The drenched mariners re-enter saying that all is lost. Everyone aboard the ship prepares for the worst. The courtiers blame the boatswain. Gonzalo longs for land: 'I would fain die a dry death' (lines 64–5).

TOP TIP (A01)

Notice how the scene's nautical language – 'main course', 'top mast', 'boatswain', 'lay her a-hold' – helps to set the scene at sea and establish the speakers as a crew of sailors. (A boatswain – pronounced 'bosun' – is a senior crewman on a ship who supervises and assigns roles to crewmembers on deck.)

CHECKPOINT 1 (A02)

How are Alonso and Sebastian related?

WHY IS THIS SCENE IMPORTANT?

A The **storm** that gives the play its **title** and sets its events in motion takes place in this scene.

B This scene is set at **sea**, and is the only scene in the play not set on the **island** itself.

C Shakespeare begins the play in **spectacular** fashion with a violent storm.

KEY LANGUAGE: HIGH DRAMA (A02)

The Tempest begins with a scene of high drama as a ship's passengers and crew suffer the effects of a dreadful storm. The first stage direction 'A tempestuous noise of thunder and lightning heard' conjures in the reader's mind the magnitude of the storm, and much of the scene's dialogue conveys the danger facing the men on board the ship and the need to take urgent action.

Throughout the scene, Shakespeare uses language to create the impression of an emergency on board ship.

Repeatedly, the playwright uses exclamations, imperatives and short sentences – 'To cabin! Silence! Trouble us not.' (lines 17–18) – to convey urgency and also a sense of the men's difficulty in making themselves heard against the noise of the storm. We can imagine that dialogue in this scene would be shouted and that the actors – particularly the ship's crew – would be constantly in motion as they follow the boatswain's instructions in a vain attempt to avert disaster.

KEY CHARACTERS: FIRST IMPRESSIONS (A01)

Shakespeare's language in this scene also communicates the inner turmoil facing the characters: their doubts, fears and disagreements. We start to learn about the personalities and temperaments of the high-ranking characters on board the ship. When the desperate Sebastian and Antonio take turns to insult the boatswain – 'you bawling, blasphemous, incharitable dog!' (Sebastian, lines 40–1), 'you whoreson insolent noisemaker!' (Antonio, lines 43–4) – we may begin to form an impression of them as judgemental and belligerent. Meanwhile Gonzalo's blackly humorous comments – 'I would fain [rather] die a dry death' (lines 64–5) – establish him not only as a loyal servant to his masters but also as a witty and thoughtful man.

KEY THEME: POWER (A02)

The cast of characters on board the ship presents us with different ways of thinking about power. On the one hand, we can see a clear and recognisable hierarchy in evidence, with royals and aristocrats (King Alonso of Naples, his brother, his son, and the Duke of Milan) served by lords, a councillor and the ship's crew. The crew also has a hierarchy and chain of command from the shipmaster, via the boatswain, down to the ship's mariners.

However there is a sense in *The Tempest* from the very outset that the disorder caused by the storm also threatens the social hierarchy, with the boatswain issuing orders to the high-ranking passengers rather than the other way around.

The first mention of the king is a reminder that there is no position of authority so senior that it gives a man protection from nature at its most violent: 'What cares these roarers [waves] for the name of king?' (lines 16–17). Shakespeare is already establishing in his audience's imagination that power takes many forms. The boatswain's sarcastic suggestion to Gonzalo that he use his 'authority' (line 23) to calm the storm further emphasises the powerlessness of the powerful in the midst of the storm.

KEY CONTEXT (A03)

In Shakespeare's time, the sound of thunder could be made by drums or by rolling a cannonball across the floor of the space above the stage, which was called the Heavens. There were also a number of techniques for creating an effect like lightning, including the use of firecrackers.

KEY CONTEXT (A03)

Shakespeare may have been influenced by real life events, in particular various accounts of a shipwreck off the coast of the Bermudas in 1609. The crew of the ship *Sea Adventure*, under the command of Sir George Somers, safely reached one of the islands and eventually rejoined the fleet in boats they built on the island.

ACT I SCENE 2: PROSPERO TELLS MIRANDA HIS STORY (LINES 1–241)

SUMMARY

- Miranda is worried about the fate of a vessel caught in the storm and implores her father to use his magic powers to 'allay' the 'wild waters' (line 2).

- Prospero reassures her that 'There's no harm done' (line 15) and that he always acts in her interests.

- Prospero explains to his daughter that it is time she knew more about her life story and her true identity. Prospero recounts the events that brought them to the island.

- Prospero explains to Miranda that he has raised the sea-storm because 'Fortune' has brought the people responsible for his overthrow 'to this shore' (lines 178–80).

- Prospero uses his magic powers to send his daughter to sleep and then summons his servant Ariel, who appears before him ready to carry out his master's instructions.

- Ariel describes to Prospero how he 'performed … the tempest' (line 194) just as Prospero instructed him. He explains that all of the ship's noble passengers jumped into the sea including Ferdinand, the king's son. Ariel reassures Prospero that they are safe and that he has 'dispersed them 'bout the isle' (line 220).

- Prospero praises Ariel but tells him there's more work to do.

TOP TIP (A02)

At over 500 lines, Act I Scene 2 is the first of many long scenes in *The Tempest*. It can be a helpful reading and revision tool to divide up the scene into smaller sections by noticing where characters enter and exit.

WHY IS THIS SCENE IMPORTANT?

A   **Prospero** and his daughter **Miranda** are introduced.

B   Prospero recounts for his daughter how they came to the **island**.

C   We learn about Prospero's **magic powers** and how **Ariel** made the **storm** happen, instructed by Prospero.

CHECKPOINT 2 (A01)

What item of clothing is Prospero wearing at the beginning of this scene and what is its significance?

KEY STRUCTURE: PROSPERO'S STORY (A02)

Shakespeare uses this scene to tell the audience about Prospero and to reveal his true identity as the rightful Duke of Milan. We learn that Antonio's ambitions led him to plot with King Alonso of Naples, Prospero's enemy, to unseat Prospero. Prospero explains how Antonio's men banished him and Miranda by taking them forcibly from Milan one night and rowing them to a 'rotten' (line 146) sailing vessel.

In amongst the treachery and cruelty recounted by Prospero, Shakespeare gives us some more positive glimpses of human nature. Prospero praises the infant Miranda's 'fortitude' (line 154) and the kindness of the Neapolitan nobleman Gonzalo who gave the pair food, fresh water, clothing and some of Prospero's books from his beloved library.

KEY CONTEXT (A03)

In line 198, Ariel describes himself appearing to the sailors on the ship as a flame. This could be a reference to the electrical weather phenomenon known as St Elmo's Fire witnessed by sailors during thunderstorms.

KEY CHARACTER: BOOKISH PROSPERO (A01)

Shakespeare presents Prospero as an intellectual figure who loves books and scholarship: 'my library/Was dukedom large enough' (lines 109–10). Indeed Prospero reflects that being immersed in his studies – 'those being all my study' (line 74) – gave his brother the opportunity to plot his overthrow. Loyal Gonzalo ensured that Prospero's books followed him into exile. Since then Prospero has spent twelve years on the island with his daughter, whom he has raised and skilfully tutored.

EXAM FOCUS: WRITING ABOUT CHARACTER (A01)

You may be asked to write in detail about a particular character. Read this example by one student commenting on the characterisation of Ariel in this scene:

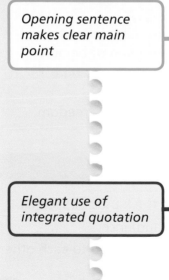

Opening sentence makes clear main point

In this scene, Shakespeare presents Ariel as a character of great vitality. A variety of verbs immediately establishes Ariel as a character who is capable of movement in air, water and fire: 'be't to fly/To swim, to dive into the fire, to ride/On the curled clouds'. The alliteration and assonance used here also convey great energy and playfulness. Ariel's freedom of movement is further suggested by his ability to 'divide/And burn in many places'. Even though Ariel is carrying out his master's instructions, Ariel's language conveys his glee in performing and recounting his magical deeds.

Language analysis shows understanding of the effect of literary features

Elegant use of integrated quotation

Now you try it:

This paragraph needs a final sentence to draw everything together, summing up Ariel's character in this scene. Start: *'In Ariel's very first exchanges with Prospero, Ariel is presented as …'*

ACT I SCENE 2: A SPIRIT, A SLAVE AND A SCHEME (LINES 242–501)

SUMMARY

- Ariel's mood becomes sullen as he reminds Prospero that he was promised his freedom.
- Prospero reminds his servant that he rescued him from the 'foul witch Sycorax' (line 258) who imprisoned Ariel in a tree for twelve years.
- Ariel asks for his master's forgiveness and Prospero sends him on another errand.
- Prospero rouses Miranda from her sleep and they look for Sycorax's son Caliban, who is Prospero's slave.
- Caliban curses Prospero and Miranda, arguing that the island is rightfully his. Prospero replies that he has treated him as well as could be expected given his behaviour.
- When Prospero threatens Caliban with terrible 'cramps' (line 369) and 'aches' (line 370), Caliban has no doubts about his master's ability to carry out his threats, and obediently leaves to fetch some fuel.
- Ferdinand appears, listening to the enchanting music that an invisible Ariel is singing and playing.
- When Miranda sees Ferdinand, she can hardly believe her eyes. His handsome and 'noble' (line 419) looks make her think he must be a 'spirit' (line 409) or 'a thing divine' (line 418).
- Prospero tells Miranda that Ferdinand has come ashore alone from the shipwreck and that he is 'goodly' (line 416) but 'something stained with grief' (lines 414–15) following his loss.
- Ferdinand sees Miranda and describes her as a 'goddess' (line 421) and a 'wonder' (line 426).
- Prospero can see his plan that Miranda and Ferdinand fall in love at first sight is working. To be sure, he accuses Ferdinand of being a 'traitor' (line 460) and threatens to 'manacle thy neck and feet together' (line 461), to which Miranda protests.
- Prospero praises Ariel for his work and promises him his freedom.

WHY IS THIS SCENE IMPORTANT?

A   We learn about **Ariel's** long imprisonment at the hands of Sycorax.

B   Prospero's slave **Caliban** is introduced to the audience.

C   **Miranda** and **Ferdinand** meet and are instantly attracted to each other.

KEY THEME: FREEDOM AND SERVITUDE

The themes of freedom and servitude are introduced when we meet two key characters who work for Prospero: the spirit Ariel and the witch's son Caliban. We also learn about the circumstances that brought the two of them under Prospero's command. Ariel and, to an even greater extent, Caliban are treated harshly by their master, although he regularly reminds

---

TOP TIP (A02)

It's helpful to highlight asides in your text – where a character speaks to the audience directly as if other characters cannot hear them. An example in this scene is when Prospero comments on the success of his plan to bring Ferdinand and Miranda together in lines 450–2. Notice how Shakespeare uses asides to show us what a character is thinking in private or, as in this example, in secret.

CHECKPOINT 3 (A01)

Who is Ferdinand's father? What does Ferdinand think has happened to him?

them of the torments from which he has freed them. In this scene, both characters alternate between complaining bitterly about their treatment and their lack of freedom, and obeying their master's instructions.

KEY THEME: MAGIC (A01)

Prospero's magic or 'art' (line 372) is shown to have dramatic and far-reaching power. In this scene, Miranda falls asleep and wakes again as a result of her father's magic. The feelings Miranda and Ferdinand have for each other are also the result of Prospero's intervention: 'they are both in either's powers' (line 450) although Shakespeare ultimately shows us that Ferdinand and Miranda's love is no magic trick but sincere and heartfelt. We have also found out in the earlier part of this scene that the storm in Act I Scene 1 was not caused by natural phenomena but was a magical occurrence performed by Ariel to his master's bidding.

KEY CHARACTER: CALIBAN (A02)

Even before Caliban is introduced to the audience, Miranda has described him as 'a villain …/I do not love to look on' (lines 309–10). When Prospero calls repeatedly for Caliban, he also refers to him in extreme terms, as 'Thou poisonous slave, got by the devil himself' (line 319). From the outset, Shakespeare is establishing that Caliban is viewed as a hideous and possibly dangerous outcast.

In this scene, Shakespeare gives the audience a first impression of Caliban as both villain and victim. While Prospero has no time for Caliban's claims and arguments, calling him a 'lying slave' (line 344), the audience has heard his grievances. However, Prospero maintains that Caliban was treated hospitably until he tried to attack Miranda and 'violate' her 'honour' (lines 347–8), an allegation of truly villainous behaviour. When Prospero threatens Caliban with painful punishments, he becomes meek and submissive once again: 'I must obey' (line 372).

AIMING HIGH: CHARACTERS' PERSPECTIVES ⭐

You will gain more marks if you can explore a character's particular perspective on events. The appearance of Ferdinand in this scene affects Miranda powerfully. Her instant attraction to Ferdinand's 'brave form' (line 411) stands in total contrast to her hatred of Caliban – 'a thing most brutish' (line 357). Prospero encourages his daughter to 'say what thou seest yond' (line 409), and this part of the scene contains several references to eyes and seeing. When Prospero reminds Miranda she has only set eyes on Caliban and Ferdinand and suggests that other men are 'angels' (line 481) compared to the one she now sees, Miranda replies that she has 'no ambition/To see a goodlier man' (line 482–3). An equally smitten Ferdinand welcomes imprisonment on the island if he can only 'Behold this maid' (line 491). But are Miranda and Ferdinand naive to trust the evidence of their own eyes?

TOP TIP (A01)

Miranda is unusual among Shakespeare's female protagonists, in that she is the sole female speaking part in the entire play. She is also unusual in that she has been confined to an island for most of her life, without access to human society, with the exception of her father and the fading memory of the 'four or five women … that tended me' (line 47). Despite this, Miranda is an educated noblewoman thanks to her 'schoolmaster' (line 172) father Prospero.

ACT II SCENE 1: COMING ASHORE (LINES 1–182)

SUMMARY

- Gonzalo is joyful that Alonso, Sebastian, Antonio and the others have survived the storm. He speaks enthusiastically and at length about the island on which they find themselves. In contrast Alonso is quieter and more sorrowful.
- Antonio and Sebastian make sarcastic comments about Gonzalo's long-winded remarks.
- Only Gonzalo notices that their clothes seem unexpectedly 'fresh' (line 70) and as if they have been 'new-dyed' (line 65), just as Ariel described in Act I Scene 2.
- The nobles talk about the wedding of Alonso's daughter Claribel to the King of Tunis from which they were returning when disaster struck. Alonso expresses regret that his daughter was married there as he fears he has lost his son in the sea-storm.
- Francisco says that he witnessed Ferdinand swimming to the shore and that he does not 'doubt/He came alive to land' (lines 121–2).
- Sebastian speaks harshly to Alonso, blaming him for recent events.
- Gonzalo criticises Sebastian's language towards the king and tries again to raise his spirits. He describes how he would turn the island into a perfect state.

WHY IS THIS SCENE IMPORTANT?

A   Just as Ariel reported, **Alonso**, **Sebastian**, **Antonio** and their attendants have now found **safety** on the **island**.

B   Although the audience knows that **Ferdinand** is safe, his father Alonso **mourns** him – an example of dramatic irony.

C   **Gonzalo's** kind and loyal nature is again in evidence but his optimism and tendency to talk are **mocked** by Antonio and Sebastian.

TOP TIP (A02)

How does Gonzalo's use of language in this scene reflect different aspects of his complex character? As the play progresses, how would you describe Gonzalo's dramatic function?

TOP TIP (A02)

This can be a difficult scene to follow on the page as Sebastian and Antonio make several sarcastic comments aside from the main conversation. As you read, work out what is being said openly, and also work out what asides Sebastian and Antonio say between themselves, and highlight this in your text.

KEY CONTEXT: IMAGINING UTOPIA (A03)

In lines 143–78 of this scene, Gonzalo describes how he would colonise the island. He imagines how he would go about building the perfect state from scratch, something philosophers and political thinkers had thought about for centuries. In lines 167–8, Gonzalo boasts that he would 'with such perfection govern …/T'excel the Golden Age'. The Golden Age is a term from Greek mythology that refers to an idealised time before work, money and law were invented when peace and harmony prevailed. Gonzalo's ideas sound attractively simple; he would do away with 'riches, poverty' (line 150) and trade – 'For no kind of traffic would I admit' (line 148–9) – and wishes that men and women could be 'idle' (line 154) and share nature's 'abundance' (line 163) communally.

Utopia, the title of a sixteenth-century novel by Sir Thomas More, literally means 'no-place', and Alonso's comment to Gonzalo 'Prithee, no more. Thou dost talk nothing to me' (line 170) contains a very similar play on words, reminding Gonzalo and the audience that his utopian dreams have no basis in reality. Sebastian and Antonio's various interruptions during Gonzalo's speech also reveal some of the paradoxes and inconsistencies of imagining the perfect state. For example, when Gonzalo says he would have 'No sovereignty', Sebastian and Antonio interject with 'Yet he would be king on't' (line 156), an important observation in a play with so much to say about power, freedom and servitude.

AIMING HIGH: ANALYSING A CHARACTER'S USE OF LANGUAGE ⭐

You will gain more marks if you can analyse a character's language closely in order to draw out a range of different uses of language and their effects. Gonzalo is one of the very first characters to speak in the play and Shakespeare presents him to us from the beginning as a thoughtful and witty man. For example Gonzalo takes comfort from the idea that the boatswain's complexion is 'perfect gallows' (I.1.30) with 'no drowning mark upon him' (I.1.29). He is here alluding to a popular proverb 'He that is born to be hanged shall never be drowned' and his comment manages to be at once reassuring, humorous and grimly realistic.

Although Gonzalo is mocked in this scene for being fussy and talkative, his words – and those of Adrian – are a typical attempt to offer comfort and hope at a difficult time: 'Here is everything advantageous to life.' (line 52). He shows wisdom and judgement in his comments to Sebastian when he criticises Alonso: 'You rub the sore,/When you should bring the plaster' (lines 138–9). His description of the society he would create on the island in this scene is pertinent to many of the play's key themes and motifs such as power, nature, exploration and the restoration of order, making Gonzalo something of a mouthpiece for important ideas within the play.

CHECKPOINT 4 (A01)

When the courtier Francisco says he has witnessed Ferdinand swimming ashore, how does Alonso respond?

KEY CONTEXT (A03)

Sir Thomas More's *Utopia* – with which Shakespeare is likely to have been familiar – describes a fictional island society. *Utopia* was first published in England in 1551 and gave rise to a literary genre of utopian writings.

ACT II SCENE 1: A PLOT TO KILL THE KING (LINES 183–327)

SUMMARY

- Ariel appears playing *'solemn music'* that puts everyone but Antonio and Sebastian to sleep.
- Antonio suggests to Sebastian that he could conspire against his brother Alonso, King of Naples and win the crown for himself.
- Sebastian says that Ferdinand and then Claribel would be next in line to the throne. Antonio encourages him to believe that Ferdinand has drowned and claims that Claribel has moved too far beyond Europe to be considered a likely heir.
- The two men discuss how Antonio supplanted Prospero as Duke of Milan and Antonio says he has no pangs of conscience about what he did.
- Antonio and Sebastian prepare to kill Alonso and Gonzalo as they sleep but Ariel reappears, sent by Prospero to protect them. His song 'While you here do snoring lie' wakes up Gonzalo, who shakes Alonso awake.
- Now everyone is awake, the lords speculate about the nature of the danger from which they seem to have had a narrow escape. They continue to search for Ferdinand, remaining on guard against 'beasts' (line 324).

CHECKPOINT 5 **A01**

From where were Alonso and his courtiers travelling when the storm struck, and why were they there?

WHY IS THIS SCENE IMPORTANT?

A **Antonio** encourages **Sebastian** to **plot** against his brother Alonso just as he successfully did against his brother Prospero.

B Prospero's **magic powers** are shown in the form of two appearances by **Ariel**, who is carrying out Prospero's instructions.

C By saving Alonso and Gonzalo, **Prospero**'s 'project' (line 299) continues.

KEY CHARACTERS: TWO PAIRS OF BROTHERS **A01**

KEY CONTEXT **A03**

Ariel's use of the word 'project' in line 299 to describe Prospero's plan has associations with alchemy, a medieval philosophy concerned with transforming base metals into gold and discovering the elixir of life (see **Part Three: Characters – Prospero**).

Once the other characters are asleep, Antonio and Sebastian's conversation takes a more conspiratorial turn. Sebastian, King Alonso's younger brother, begins to warm to Antonio's idea that would see him with 'a crown/ Dropping upon thy head' (lines 207–8). But it is not only King Alonso who stands in Sebastian's way; his son and heir Ferdinand and daughter Claribel, now married to the King of Tunis, also stop Sebastian becoming the King of Naples. Our impression of Sebastian is that he is capable of ambition and ruthlessness but lacks Antonio's drive. By the end of the scene, Antonio has succeeded in convincing Sebastian to mimic his actions: 'As thou got'st Milan,/I'll come by Naples' (lines 291–2).

The parallels between Sebastian's and Antonio's situations are a key element in convincing Sebastian to turn envy into action. Antonio brags about his success: 'look how well his garments sit upon me/Much feater than before' (lines 272–273), making usurpation seem achievable and desirable and dismissing Sebastian's concerns about 'conscience' (line 275). We obtain a frightening glimpse into the mind of the unscrupulous Antonio, who appears to show no remorse for his treatment of his own brother Prospero, the rightful Duke of Milan.

KEY LANGUAGE: METAPHOR (A02)

Shakespeare uses recurring images in this scene that are also echoed elsewhere in the play. Sleep is a powerful **metaphor** used by Antonio in his attempts to persuade Sebastian into treacherous action: 'Thou let'st thy fortune sleep – die, rather' (line 215). He describes Sebastian as keeping his eyes closed rather than being alert to opportunities that present themselves. Antonio also builds on **imagery** used by Sebastian to argue his point: when Sebastian describes himself as 'standing water' (line 220), Antonio replies that he will 'teach him how to flow' (line 221). While Antonio makes powerful use of these images in this scene, his efforts are ultimately thwarted by Ariel's reappearance. In the end it is Prospero's powers – over water (to create the storm) and over sleep (in both this and the previous scene) – that Shakespeare places firmly in our minds.

CHECKPOINT 6 (A01)

What do Sebastian and Antonio tell Alonso they will do while he is sleeping?

TOP TIP (A01)

Find as much evidence as you can about Antonio's ambitious nature. You could use quotations to chart his growing ambition as he sets his sights on Alonso in Act II Scene 1 and again in Act III Scene 3.

EXAM FOCUS: WRITING ABOUT PERSUASIVE LANGUAGE (A02) ✏

You may be asked to write in detail about a character's skilful use of language in *The Tempest*. Read this example by one student analysing the language Antonio uses here:

Precise use of language to argue main point of paragraph

Antonio uses language to persuade and corrupt Sebastian in this scene. Antonio uses mystical language to describe his vision: 'methinks I see it in thy face,/What thou shouldst be' (lines 205-6). Antonio also addresses Sebastian as a man of importance – 'Worthy Sebastian' (line 204), 'Noble Sebastian' (line 214) – but describes Alonso as worthless: 'Here lies your brother,/No better than the earth he lies upon'. He also speaks enthusiastically about the attractions of power: 'My brother's servants/Were then my fellows; now they are my men' (lines 273-4).

Good understanding of the effects of language illustrated by short, well-chosen quotations

Now you try it:

This paragraph needs a final sentence to draw everything together. Add a sentence that describes the combined effects of Antonio's language choices on Sebastian. Start: *Over the course of the two men's conversation, Shakespeare shows how …*

ACT II SCENE 2: CALIBAN, TRINCULO AND STEPHANO FIND EACH OTHER

CHECKPOINT 7 **A01**

What do Trinculo and Stephano say they did to make their escape to the island during the storm?

SUMMARY

- A thunderstorm is brewing. Caliban enters carrying wood and cursing his master Prospero.
- Caliban notices Trinculo and, thinking that Trinculo is another of Prospero's spirits who has come to torment him, hides under a cloak.
- Trinculo is looking for somewhere to hide from the coming storm. He notices Caliban and wonders what kind of creature he is. He decides to creep under Caliban's cloak.
- Stephano enters singing shanties and drinking wine from a bottle. Caliban, believing he is being tormented by a spirit, cries out from under the cloak and Stephano thinks he must be 'some monster of the isle with four legs' (line 65).
- Stephano gives Caliban wine which, at first, he spits out, but which he later describes as 'celestial liquor' (line 117). He becomes increasingly drunk.
- Trinculo recognises Stephano's voice but is puzzled as he thought he had drowned. Stephano now thinks that the four-legged creature has two mouths (and hence two voices), and calls him 'a devil' (line 98).
- Stephano pulls Trinculo out from under the cloak and they exchange stories about how they survived the storm.
- Caliban views Trinculo and Stephano as 'fine things, an if they be not sprites' (line 116). He believes Stephano when he says he used to be the 'Man i'th'Moon' (line 138) and views him as a godlike figure. They, in turn, view Caliban as a 'credulous' (line 146) and 'ridiculous' (line 165) figure.
- Caliban expresses devotion to Stephano and promises to show him every inch of the island and to share all of his local knowledge.

TOP TIP **A02**

Ironically, in the scene that follows, Ferdinand enters carrying wood for Prospero just as Caliban does at the beginning of this scene. Here Shakespeare is exploring parallels between the two characters' situations but also reminding us of the immense differences between their status and prospects.

TOP TIP **A02**

Much of the scene is written in prose appropriate to Stephano and Trinculo's lowly status. However, Caliban's language blends verse and prose in a distinctive way.

WHY IS THIS SCENE IMPORTANT?

A The focus moves from the **noble** survivors of the shipwreck to **lower-class** servants: Alonso's butler (Stephano) and jester (Trinculo).

B With its visual humour, drunken behaviour and cases of mistaken identity, this is a scene rich in **comedy**.

C **Caliban**, dissatisfied with being Prospero's slave, looks to **Stephano** to be his new master.

KEY STRUCTURE: PARALLELS AND CONTRASTS **A02**

As the characters in the play come ashore, Shakespeare uses each change of scene to move the audience's focus between the various survivors and to establish some parallels and contrasts between them. Whereas in the previous scene Sebastian and Antonio plotted Alonso's overthrow, now Caliban seeks to be rid of his master Prospero. The tragic irony of Caliban's situation is that he appears to equate 'freedom' (line 185) with getting 'a new master' (line 184). This is in stark contrast to how the other characters describe their ambitions. Earlier, Prospero describes his dishonourable brother Antonio as 'so dry [thirsty] … for sway [power]' (I.2.112) that he would stop at nothing to obtain the 'Absolute' (I.2.109) power he craved.

AIMING HIGH: AN UPSIDE-DOWN WORLD

Notice how from the very beginning of the play, when the seamen had to give firm instructions to the noblemen during the storm, the tempest has turned the social order upside down. Antonio's seizure of power from Prospero can be seen as having disturbed the natural order of things in the first place; Shakespeare is concerned with the sequence of events Prospero has set in motion to restore order, on which 'my zenith doth depend' (I.2.181). In the meantime, kings and dukes are washed up on the shore along with butlers and jesters, and Shakespeare creates both comedy and social commentary from the unlikely events and situations that follow.

KEY QUOTATION: AN IMAGINED INHERITANCE **A01**

Near the end of this scene, Stephano comments that 'the King and all our company else being drowned, we will inherit here' (line 175). He indulgently imagines what he and Trinculo might 'inherit' if they are the only two survivors and rise to positions of power as a consequence. Shakespeare is illustrating that the desire to discover – and have power over – places and people is a universal human characteristic – from Sebastian's openness to the idea of ousting his own brother, to Gonzalo's reimagining of the newly discovered island as a civilised utopia.

REVISION FOCUS: COMEDY

How does Shakespeare succeed in making this a humorous scene? What advice would you give to the actors playing Stephano and Trinculo? Make a list of the elements of this scene (in terms of plotting, characterisation, stagecraft and language) that contribute to the scene's comedy and support your points with textual evidence.

KEY CONTEXT **A03**

Stephano and Trinculo repeatedly refer to Caliban as a 'mooncalf'. The earliest recorded usage of this word dates from 1565. The word can be used to mean a misshapen animal or human birth, a fool or a person under the influence of the Moon. It used to be thought that there was a relationship between abnormalities in newborns and the phases of the Moon.

CHECKPOINT 8 **A01**

In his song, which four tasks does Caliban say he would never need to do again for Prospero?

ACT III SCENE 1: FERDINAND AND MIRANDA DECLARE THEIR LOVE

SUMMARY

- Ferdinand is gathering wood for Prospero. He pauses to make admiring comments about his 'gentle' (line 8) mistress and her ability to make 'my labours pleasures' (line 7) before resuming his work.
- Miranda appears. She urges Ferdinand to take some rest and offers to help him with his work though he will not let her labour 'While I sit lazy by' (line 28).
- Although Miranda says that her father is 'hard at study' (line 20) and will be gone three hours, Prospero has followed Miranda and is hidden from Miranda and Ferdinand's view but visible to the audience. He speaks using asides to comment on the success of his plan.
- Miranda tells Ferdinand her name and Ferdinand praises her many virtues. Miranda replies that she 'would not wish/Any companion in the world but you' (lines 54–5).
- Miranda and Ferdinand profess their love and desire to marry each other.
- They part and Prospero returns to his 'business' (line 96).

WHY IS THIS SCENE IMPORTANT?

A This scene confirms for the audience that **Miranda** and **Ferdinand** are truly in **love**.

B We learn more about Ferdinand and Miranda's **characters**.

C **Prospero's scheme** – that requires Ferdinand, son and heir to the King of Naples and Miranda, daughter and heir of the rightful Duke of Milan to **marry** – continues to go to plan.

TOP TIP: WRITING ABOUT LOVE AND MARRIAGE (A03)

In this scene, Ferdinand and Miranda make several references to each other's worth and their own lowliness by comparison: 'My heart fly to your service' (line 65), 'mine unworthiness' (line 77), 'I thus humble ever' (line 87). Before meeting Miranda, Ferdinand found 'some defect' (line 44) in women he had seen, but he believes Miranda to be 'created/Of every creature's best' (lines 47–8) with qualities that go beyond attractive looks and seductive words. Miranda says her 'modesty' is 'The jewel in my dower [marriage gifts]' (lines 53–4), referring to the importance above of all else of her honour or virginity upon entering a marriage arrangement. She also comments that her father would not be happy to hear her 'prattle …/Something too wildly' (lines 57–8), further suggesting that Prospero has been strict in his advice about her behaviour with men, in keeping with views of the time.

Ferdinand mentions in line 59 that he is 'in my condition/A prince' and we are reminded of the political implications of marriage between the two households. However, unlike the purely political marriage that took place between the King of Tunis and Ferdinand's sister Claribel, the match between Ferdinand and Miranda is a loving one.

CHECKPOINT 9 (A01)

What had Miranda been instructed by her father not to say to Ferdinand?

EXAM FOCUS: WRITING ABOUT RELATIONSHIPS (A01) ✏

You may be asked to write in detail about the relationship between characters. Read this example by one student commenting on the developing relationship between Ferdinand and Miranda in this scene:

> In this scene, Ferdinand and Miranda speak sincerely about their love and desire to be married. Unlike Ferdinand who has 'liked several women' (line 43), Miranda is unworldly. As she explains, she knows nothing of men and women apart from her father, Ferdinand and her own reflection in the mirror, but cannot imagine 'a shape/ Besides yourself, to like of' (lines 56-7). Ferdinand expresses his love for Miranda in similar terms, describing her as: 'So perfect and so peerless' (line 47). The seriousness of their words to each other in this scene begins to resemble - and foreshadow - the exchange of marriage vows.

Appropriate choice of sentence structure for writing about a contrast

Short quotation integrated into sentence

Brief reference to their planned wedding in Naples

Now you try it:

This paragraph needs a final sentence to draw everything together. Add one that explains how Shakespeare conveys the intensity of Miranda and Ferdinand's feelings for one another in this scene. Start: *In this scene, Shakespeare shows the audience…*

ACT III SCENE 2: A PLOT TO KILL PROSPERO

SUMMARY

- Stephano and Trinculo have been drinking and Stephano commands Caliban to drink with them.

- Caliban tells Stephano about how Prospero 'by his cunning hath cheated me of the island' (lines 42–3). Trinculo mocks Caliban who appeals to Stephano to intervene.

- An invisible Ariel enters and imitates Trinculo's voice, accusing Caliban of lying. Caliban appeals to Stephano to punish Trinculo for his impertinence.

- Caliban tells Stephano that Prospero took the island from him 'by sorcery' (line 52) and says that if Stephano were to kill Prospero, he would be the island's ruler and Caliban would be his willing servant.

- Stephano tells Trinculo he will strike him if he interrupts again. Ariel speaks in Trinculo's voice and Stephano carries out his threat. Trinculo protests and curses Stephano.

- Caliban describes various methods of killing Prospero that Stephano could employ. He also emphasises the importance of stealing Prospero's 'books, for without them/He's but a sot as I am' (lines 93–4) and tempts Stephano with the idea that he could marry Prospero's beautiful daughter. Stephano agrees to kill Prospero in his sleep.

- They all start to sing a song but cannot remember the tune. Unseen, Ariel plays the tune to the men's astonishment. Caliban tells his companions not to be afraid of this ghostly playing as 'the isle is full of noises' (line 136).

CHECKPOINT 10 (A01)

Which implements does Caliban suggest to Stephano that he could use to kill Prospero?

KEY CONTEXT (A03)

Shakespeare includes many references to music in *The Tempest*. In this particular scene, Ariel plays a tune on the pipe and *'tabor'* – a small drum. 'Airs' (line 137) means songs or melodies while a 'catch' (line 118) is a more intricate composition for three or more voices.

WHY IS THIS SCENE IMPORTANT?

A The audience's attention returns to **Stephano**, **Trinculo** and **Caliban**.

B **Stephano** is enjoying his **power** over **Caliban**, and parts of the scene parody the language of royal courts.

C Shakespeare draws a **parallel** between Caliban and Stephano's **plot** to kill **Prospero** in his sleep and Antonio and Sebastian's plan to kill **Alonso** in his sleep.

KEY LANGUAGE: INSULTS, THREATS AND CURSES (A02)

This scene's colourful language aids our understanding of characters and relationships as well as providing humour. During their verbal sparrings, Trinculo calls Caliban 'thou debauched fish thou' (line 26) and Caliban later calls Trinculo 'thou jesting monkey thou' (line 45), each man using animal references to belittle the other. Both Caliban and Trinculo mock each other's physical appearance; Caliban's insults 'pied ninny' and 'scurvy patch' (line 63) relate to the fact that Trinculo is a jester and wears a jester's clothes or motley.

This animated scene also contains many curses and threats, for example when Stephano tells Trinculo that if he interrupts again, 'I will supplant some of your teeth' (line 49). He later threatens to 'make a stockfish of thee' (lines 70–1), meaning that he will beat him. Shakespeare's very physical diction in this scene and his use of short phrases and sentences, including many exclamations, create the effect of language being used as a weapon – not only to insult, curse and threaten but also, as Caliban skilfully does with Stephano, to goad another person into action.

KEY CONTEXT: SHAKESPEARE'S STAGE SKILLS

There are numerous ways in which Shakespeare makes imaginative use of Elizabethan/Jacobean theatre design and stage skills in this play. In this scene, Caliban says that 'The clouds methought would open, and show riches/Ready to drop upon me' (lines 142–3) and it was common for clouds to be painted on the wooden ceilings of outdoor theatres (above the stage itself) in Shakespeare's time. In private indoor theatres, the entire ceiling might be decorated with blue skies, clouds, and other aerial motifs. In Act III Scene 3, Shakespeare's stage directions refer to a *'quaint device'* – perhaps a tabletop that flips over – that makes the banquet disappear. At the beginning of the same scene, Prospero appears *'on the top'* by which Shakespeare probably meant he appears in the musician's gallery above the stage, thus visible to the audience but capable of staying hidden from other characters. When the goddess *'Juno descends'* in Act IV Scene 1, Shakespeare might be envisaging some kind of contraption to lower the actor to the stage from the 'heavens' above.

TOP TIP: WRITING ABOUT SPEECH (A02)

It's important that you think about the sound of Shakespeare's language as well as its meaning. In stark contrast to the bitter arguments and name-calling with which the scene began, Shakespeare gives Caliban a lyrical speech (lines 136–44) about the island's strange sounds towards the end of the scene. The rhythms of this speech are closer to iambic pentameter than anything else in the scene and the sounds are musical. Look for examples in the speech of alliteration, assonance, repetition and sibilance and consider their effects on the listener.

KEY CONTEXT (A03)

When Caliban calls Trinculo 'Thou scurvy patch!' in line 63, he is alluding to Cardinal Wolsey's jester Sexton known by his nickname 'Patch' meaning fool. Cardinal Wolsey had been one of Henry VIII's chief advisors before falling out of favour with the king.

ACT III SCENE 3: PROSPERO'S REVENGE

SUMMARY

- Alonso, Sebastian, Antonio and Gonzalo are exhausted after searching for Ferdinand. Alonso has lost all hope of finding his son.
- Antonio and Sebastian privately plan to kill Alonso.
- *'Solemn and strange music'* is heard. Dancing *'shapes'* appear with a banquet, and depart. Prospero also appears overhead but is only visible to the audience.
- Sebastian notes that the dancing shapes 'have left their viands behind' (line 41) and suggests that they eat the food, but a winged Ariel enters *'like a harpy'* and makes the food disappear. The lords draw their swords but Ariel has made them too heavy to lift.
- Ariel delivers a speech written by Prospero in which he addresses Alonso, Antonio and Sebastian as 'three men of sin' (line 53) because they 'did supplant good Prospero' (line 70). He explains how the storm and the loss of Ferdinand are the gods' judgement for their 'foul deed' (line 72) and that only by repenting and leading 'a clear life' (line 82) can they escape divine wrath.
- Ariel vanishes and the dancing shapes reappear to musical accompaniment and carry away the banqueting table.
- Prospero praises Ariel for performing his duties and leaves to visit Ferdinand and Miranda.
- Alonso, Antonio and Sebastian react to what they have witnessed before exiting. While Alonso is guilt-ridden, Antonio and Sebastian are ready to 'fight' (line 103) the spirits. Gonzalo asks the younger members of the party to pursue his masters to 'hinder them from what this ecstasy [madness]/May now provoke them to' (lines 108–9).

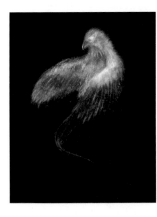

KEY CONTEXT A03

The two mythical beasts mentioned by Sebastian in this scene – 'unicorns' (line 22) and the 'phoenix' (line 23) – featured widely in travel writing during the Middle Ages and Renaissance.

WHY IS THIS SCENE IMPORTANT?

A **Prospero's** plan is reaching a **climax**, as he confronts those responsible for his overthrow with their wrongdoing.

B Prospero stages an elaborate **performance** with a banquet, music, dancing figures and a long speech delivered by **Ariel**.

C **Tension** mounts as **Gonzalo** fears his masters' guilt might motivate them to do something rash.

TOP TIP: WRITING ABOUT ARIEL (A02)

In this scene, Prospero stages an elaborate spectacle with Ariel playing a harpy. His mastery over thunder and lightning, the dancing shapes and the appearance and disappearance of the banquet demonstrates the formidable extent of his powers compared with those of the shipwrecked lords who are now truly at his mercy.

KEY CONTEXT: FATE AND JUDGEMENT (A03)

When Ariel enters in this scene, Shakespeare tells us that he wears wings and looks *'like a harpy'*, a mythical creature with the face and breasts of a woman and the talons and wings of a bird. Harpies appear in the legendary story of Aeneas told by Virgil (See **Part Four: Contexts – Classical Myths and Legends**) and are associated with punishment meted out by the gods. Similarly, in this scene, Ariel says that he and his *'fellows'* (line 60) are *'ministers of Fate'* (line 61) speaking for the *'deities'* (line 73) and pronouncing their judgement on those who have behaved unjustly and harmfully towards Prospero *'and his innocent child'* (line 72).

KEY QUOTATION: THE EFFECTS OF GUILT (A01)

At the end of this scene, Gonzalo concludes that *'All three of them are desperate. Their great guilt,/Like poison given to work a great time after,/Now 'gins to bite their spirits'* (lines 104–6). Gonzalo understands how knowledge of their own wrongdoing has affected Alonso, Antonio and Sebastian, albeit in different ways. Using the **simile** of 'poison', Shakespeare suggests that in committing harmful actions, the three men have ultimately harmed themselves too. In Alonso's case, the effect is devastating: *'O, it is monstrous, monstrous!'* (line 105) and the only future he can see for himself is to *'lie mudded'* (line 102) on the seabed with his son. There is no such soul-searching for Antonio and Sebastian, however. They remain defiant.

REVISION FOCUS: CHANGES OF FORTUNE

The fortunes of many characters change dramatically during *The Tempest* and transformation is an important **motif**. Make notes about how each character's fortunes change throughout the play. Think about their status and rank and also about what motivates and drives each character.

TOP TIP (A02)

Notice how Shakespeare achieves the grand style of Ariel's long speech (lines 53–82) using formal words and phrases and long and complex sentences. You could compare and contrast this speech with the more lively and natural language Ariel uses when he describes to Prospero how he performed the tempest in Act I Scene 2.

CHECKPOINT 11 (A01)

Which key character in this scene does not witness the spectacle and how do we know?

ACT IV SCENE 1 (LINES 1–145): A THEATRICAL CELEBRATION

SUMMARY

- Prospero says he will gladly give Ferdinand his daughter Miranda's hand in marriage but repeatedly warns him against sexual relations before they are married. Ferdinand reassures him.

- Prospero tells Ariel he wishes to show the 'young couple/Some vanity of mine art' (lines 40–1). To celebrate their engagement, he shows the lovers a masque in which spirits playing goddesses from classical mythology speak, and there is 'soft music' and singing.

- During the masque, the goddesses bless the engaged couple and wish that they may be 'prosperous' and 'honoured in thy issue' (lines 104–5).

- A delighted Ferdinand comments that the masque is 'a most majestic vision' (line 118) and 'harmonious charmingly' (line 119).

- Nymphs and reapers enter and perform a graceful rustic dance.

- The masque ends suddenly with Prospero appearing to Ferdinand and Miranda 'touched with anger so distempered' (line 145) as he remembers the unfinished business of the 'foul conspiracy' against him plotted by Caliban and his 'confederates' (line 140).

WHY IS THIS SCENE IMPORTANT?

A Prospero agrees to let Ferdinand **marry** his daughter.

B The masque formally marks the couple's **engagement** and celebrates their **love**, forthcoming **marriage** and hopes of having **children** to succeed them.

C The **mood** changes after the masque as Prospero is reminded of the plot against him.

KEY CONTEXT: CLASSICAL GODDESSES **A03**

The three classical goddesses each have a symbolic connection with the purpose of the masque. Iris represents the rainbow and is a messenger between the gods in Heaven and humans on Earth. Ceres, whose daughter Proserpine was abducted by Pluto or 'Dis' (line 89) and taken to the Underworld, is associated with fertility, agriculture and the harvest, while Juno is the goddess of marriage and childbirth.

KEY FORM: MASQUE **A02**

A masque was a form of courtly entertainment that was popular in the sixteenth and seventeenth centuries. Masques included dialogue, dancing and music and often had their roots in classical myths and fables. Costumes and set designs were elaborate and rural settings were common.

Shakespeare's masque in this scene reflects all of these conventions. The masque opens with Iris instructing Ceres to leave behind a pastoral setting that is described in idyllic terms for over ten lines: 'Thy turfy mountains, where live nibbling sheep … Thy banks with peonied and twillèd brims' (lines 62–4). Ceres refers to 'this short-grassed green' (line 83) (masques were often performed on green baize cloth), and the masque ends with a festive formal dance.

Masques were traditionally private in nature. The characters often had an allegorical significance for the royal or aristocratic patrons for whom the entertainment was written and staged. The masque in *The Tempest* has been created and performed to bless and celebrate the engagement of Miranda and Ferdinand, whose loving union is mentioned frequently: 'a contract of true love' (line 84), 'Go with me to bless this twain' (line 104), 'Juno sings her blessings on you' (line 109). A crucial difference between Prospero's masque and a courtly masque is that Prospero's one is performed not by courtiers and by professional actors and singers but by spirits. Here Shakespeare is showing the audience that life on the island mirrors but is not the same as courtly life.

CHECKPOINT 12 A01

How does the goddess Juno make her entrance?

TOP TIP A01

Notice how the masque itself (lines 60–138) is written entirely in rhyming couplets, creating a different effect to the more naturalistic blank verse used much more widely in the play.

CHECKPOINT 13 **A01**

Who did Ariel say he presented in the masque?

KEY CONTEXT **A03**

In the Renaissance, additional masques called anti-masques were performed for comic or grotesque contrast. How does the episode involving Caliban, Stephano and Trinculo in this scene create a contrast with the masque that precedes it?

ACT IV SCENE 1 (LINES 146–265): THE PLOT AGAINST PROSPERO IS FOILED

SUMMARY

- Prospero explains that the masque has ended and says he will seek rest and repose 'to still my beating mind' (line 163). Ferdinand and Miranda leave and Prospero summons Ariel.

- Ariel tells Prospero about how he 'charmed' (line 178) the ears of Stephano, Trinculo and Caliban and has led them 'I'th'filthy-mantled pool beyond your cell' (line 182). Prospero now asks him to lure them with showy trinkets and items of clothing so as to catch them in the act of stealing from his cell.

- Stephano, Trinculo and Caliban appear on stage. Stephano and Trinculo are indeed distracted by what they can steal, whereas Caliban is impatient to 'do the murder first' (line 232).

- There is 'a noise of hunters' and spirits in the shape of dogs and hounds drive out and pursue the three intruders.

- Prospero tells Ariel that they both will soon find rest from their labours.

WHY IS THIS SCENE IMPORTANT?

A **Prospero** speaks movingly about the insubstantial nature of theatre and of life itself.

B Stephano, Trinculo and Caliban's **plot** against Prospero is successfully foiled and they are **punished**.

C The sense of an approaching **ending** pervades this scene: Prospero's magical labours 'Shortly shall … end' (line 163) as will Ariel's service to Prospero and the play itself.

TOP TIP: WRITING ABOUT PERFORMANCE **A03**

Shakespeare's dialogue in lines 194–253 contains several performance clues. What advice might you give to the actors playing Stephano, Trinculo and Caliban about their delivery of these lines? You could also consider the whereabouts of Prospero at this point in the play, and how you would stage the entrance of the 'divers Spirits in shape of dogs and hounds, hunting them about, Prospero and Ariel setting them on'.

KEY QUOTATION: THE END OF THE ILLUSION (A01)

Prospero says to Ferdinand that 'Our revels [festivities] now are ended' (line 148) and goes on to speak at some length about the impermanence of things. He refers not only to the gorgeous 'vision' (line 151) or 'pageant' (line 155) they have just witnessed but also to life itself in the sentence 'We are such stuff/As dreams are made on, and our little life/Is rounded with a sleep' (lines 156–8). His words have also been taken as a metaphor for the experience of watching a play at the theatre. In his list of architectural splendours that can be created on stage only to be hoisted away or torn down, he mentions 'the great globe itself' (line 153). Here 'globe' means the whole world but is also a pun on the name of Shakespeare's famous theatre in Bankside, London.

CHECKPOINT 14 (A01)

How are Caliban, Stephano and Trinculo to be punished?

EXAM FOCUS: WRITING ABOUT PROSPERO (A01)

You may be asked to write in detail about Prospero. Read this example by one student commenting on Shakespeare's characterisation of Prospero as the play reaches its climax:

> Throughout the play, Shakespeare has shown us many different facets of Prospero's character and it could be argued that they are all in evidence within this scene: he is fatherly, stern, intellectual, fond, proud and anxious. In this scene we also see a philosophical and more inward-looking quality as Prospero begins to anticipate the end of his 'project' and his 'art': 'Yea, all which it inherit, shall dissolve.' Shakespeare uses many words to describe the loss of something that had previously been something of substance within one's grasp: 'melted', 'baseless', 'insubstantial,' 'faded'.

Precise and concise list of adjectives to indicate a range of points

Deeper analysis

Patterns in language and imagery identified

Now you try it:

This paragraph needs a sentence explaining how Prospero ends the speech and how this contrasts with his statements at the beginning.

ACT V SCENE 1 (LINES 1–134): PROSPERO RENOUNCES MAGIC

SUMMARY

- Prospero enters in his magic robes and says to Ariel that his project 'does … gather to a head' (line 1).
- Prospero asks Ariel about 'the King and's followers' (line 7) and Ariel describes their pitiful state in confinement.
- Alone on stage, Prospero draws a circle on the ground with his staff. In a long speech, he declares that he renounces his magic and pledges to break his staff and drown his book.
- Ariel brings Alonso, Gonzalo, Sebastian, Antonio, Adrian and Francisco to his master. They enter the circle and stand there, still under the influence of Prospero's spell, though the charm is beginning to wear off and the men's 'understanding' (line 79) is starting to 'swell' (line 80).
- Prospero speaks to each of them though they are not yet aware of him. Ariel helps Prospero remove his robes and get dressed in courtly attire so that he appears to his captives as the Duke of Milan.
- Ariel sings in anticipation of winning his freedom. Prospero tells him he 'shall miss/Thee, but thou shalt have freedom' (lines 95–6) and commands him to go to the king's ship and bring to him the ship's master and boatswain.
- Alonso and the others become conscious of their surroundings but continue to feel uneasy and confused.
- Alonso tells Prospero that 'Thy dukedom I resign' (line 117), even though he cannot believe that Prospero is alive and resident on the island.
- Prospero's greeting to Gonzalo is tender and sincere and he welcomes his 'friends' (line 125) to the island but warns Sebastian and Antonio in an aside that he could prove them 'traitors' (line 128).
- Before the assembled company, Prospero tells Antonio that he forgives him but that he 'must restore' (line 133) his dukedom to him.

WHY IS THIS SCENE IMPORTANT?

A **Prospero** renounces his **magic powers**.

B Prospero's **political powers** are returned to him by King **Alonso**.

C Alonso is **penitent** and asks Prospero to **pardon** his wrongs.

KEY THEMES: RECONCILIATION

At the beginning of this scene, Ariel tells Prospero that Alonso, Antonio and Sebastian are all 'distracted [absent minded]' (line 12) and that the other men are all 'Brimful of sorrow and dismay' (line 14). Movingly, he describes Gonzalo's tears running 'down his beard like winter's drops [of rain or dew]' (lines 16–17). Prospero is moved by Ariel's description and explains that he will be led by 'virtue' (line 28) and 'my nobler reason'

KEY CONTEXT **A03**

In Shakespeare's time, a boy actor (rather than a grown man) probably played the part of Ariel. Although Ariel is referred to in the text as male, the parts he plays (Ceres, harpy) are female. Since then, Ariel has been played by both male and female actors.

(line 26) rather than 'vengeance' (line 28) and 'fury' (line 26) in his dealings with the three men who have wronged him.

However, while Alonso fully accepts he has done wrong, Sebastian and Antonio have less to say for themselves in this final scene. Prospero, who had said in lines 28–30 that 'They being penitent,/The sole drift of my purpose doth extend/Not a frown further', in other words, it is Antonio's repentance that is important to him, ultimately has his dukedom returned to him because Alonso has decreed it must be so. The extent to which Prospero and Alonso are truly – as opposed to grudgingly – reconciled is left open to interpretation.

TOP TIP: WRITING ABOUT PROSPERO'S POWERS (A01)

In lines 35–50, Prospero's speech in this scene beginning 'Ye elves of hills, brooks, standing lakes, and groves' draws extensively on a speech by the sorceress Medea in the Roman poet Ovid's *Metamorphoses* in which she describes the extent of her magic powers. The speech would have been well known to audiences at the time both in its original Latin and in translation. (See also **Part Four: Contexts – Classical Myths and Legends**.)

Before renouncing his 'potent art' (line 50), Prospero also lists many magical accomplishments. As you reread this passage (lines 34–50), try comparing his speech with the speech by Ovid that inspired it, and with what we already know about Prospero's magical powers in the play. Notice for example how Prospero talks about his powers here in the past tense.

CHECKPOINT 15 (A01)

What does Prospero say he will do with his broken staff?

REVISION FOCUS: THE POWER OF MUSIC

In line 52, Prospero requires 'Some heavenly music' to awake the senses of his sleeping captives. In Shakespeare's time, people believed in the harmony of the spheres: the idea that music helped to keep the universe ordered and the individual mind healthy.

Make notes about this concept and its relevance to the play. Where else in *The Tempest* does Shakespeare show music having a beneficial effect on the mind?

ACT V SCENE 1 (LINES 134–319): REUNION AND RETURN

SUMMARY

- Alonso tells Prospero about the loss of his son in the storm. Prospero expresses his sympathy and says that his daughter too is lost 'In this last tempest' (line 153). Ironically, Alonso wishes that his son and Prospero's daughter could be 'living in Naples/The king and queen there!' (lines 149–50).

- Ferdinand and his father are reunited and Alonso warmly welcomes Miranda to their family. In lines 205–13, Gonzalo summarises the several ways in which happy outcomes have been reached and order restored.

- Ariel returns with the boatswain and the ship's master. They bring news that they awoke from a deep sleep to find the king's ship was rigged and seaworthy. Prospero tells Ariel that he has performed this task 'Bravely' (line 242) and that he will be granted his freedom.

- Prospero then instructs Ariel to free Caliban, Stephano and Trinculo. Ariel re-enters with the three men 'in their stolen apparel'. Prospero explains that they stole from him and plotted to take his life. He acknowledges responsibility for Caliban who craves his forgiveness. He admits he was 'a thrice double ass … to take this drunkard for a god' (lines 296–7).

- Prospero invites King Alonso and his retinue to rest in his humble dwelling overnight where, he says, he will tell them 'the story of my life' (line 305). In the morning they will sail to Naples for Miranda and Ferdinand's wedding.

- Prospero enlists the help of Ariel as he promises good weather and calm seas for the voyage home. Then he tells Ariel, 'to the elements/Be free, and fare thou well' (lines 318–19).

WHY IS THIS SCENE IMPORTANT?

A **Ferdinand** and his father **Alonso** are reunited and Alonso welcomes news of his son's engagement to **Miranda**.

B **Forgiveness** also extends towards the thieving and plotting of **Stephano**, **Trinculo** and **Caliban**.

C There is **happiness** as Miranda and Ferdinand's **wedding** is planned in Naples. **Prospero** plans to return to Milan and **Ariel** receives his **freedom**.

TOP TIP (A02)

Notice how Prospero sums up his story in three lines. He is both 'that very duke/Which was thrust forth of Milan' (lines 159–60) and the lord of the island 'where you [Alonso] were wrecked' (line 161). He promises a 'wonder to content ye/As much to me my dukedom' (lines 170–1) and reveals at the back of the stage Ferdinand and Miranda playing a game of chess.

TOP TIP: METAPHORS **A03**

Chess was a popular game in Elizabethan and Jacobean times and was played by aristocrats and royalty. Indeed the game itself has at its heart the metaphor of conflict between royal households. The conversation between Ferdinand and Miranda in this scene is about their game. However, Shakespeare is also reminding us that the two characters will become king and queen and be responsible for ruling and defending their kingdom and their own positions of power.

KEY QUOTATION: MIRANDA'S NEW WORLD **A01**

Miranda's exclamation 'O brave new world,/That has such people in't!' (lines 183–4) is her response to setting eyes on more people than she had ever previously seen on the island. Shakespeare's language captures her excitement but possibly also her wariness about entering society where disputes and betrayals are rife. Her words famously gave Aldous Huxley the title for his futuristic novel *Brave New World* published in 1932.

CHECKPOINT 16 **A01**

What task does Prospero assign to Caliban and his fellow conspirators?

AIMING HIGH: WONDER

You will gain more marks if you can write in an insightful way about words and ideas that appear to have a particular significance for Shakespeare in this play. For example, the word 'wonder' is used several times. Ferdinand uses 'wonder' to describe Miranda in Act I Scene 2 when he first sees her and 'wonder' is also the literal meaning of the name Shakespeare has coined for her. In Act V Scene 1, Prospero uses 'wonder' just before he reveals Ferdinand and Miranda to an amazed Alonso – 'At least bring forth a wonder to content ye/As much as me my dukedom' (V.1.170–1) – and Miranda exclaims the word – 'O wonder!' – as she sees 'How beauteous mankind is!' (line 183).

The play also reminds us of how powerful 'wonder' is; repeatedly, Prospero uses his powers to bring about his desired outcome through awe-inspiring events that disturb and deceive the senses. Earlier in the final scene Gonzalo says fearfully that 'All torment, trouble, wonder, and amazement/ Inhabits here' (V.1.104–5) and when Prospero addresses him, Gonzalo finds it impossible at first to know 'Whether this be/ Or be not' (V.1.122–3). Look for further instances in the play where characters become, as Prospero says to Alonso and the lords, 'jostled from your senses' (V.1.158) and analyse the language Shakespeare uses.

EPILOGUE: PROSPERO'S FAREWELL

SUMMARY

- Prospero remains on the stage and speaks directly to the audience. He says his magic powers are now 'all o'erthrown' (line 1) and his human powers are 'faint' (line 3).
- He summarises what he has achieved in the course of the play: 'I have my dukedom got/And pardoned the deceiver' (lines 6–7), referring to his brother Antonio.
- He asks the audience to release him from their 'spell' (line 8) and send him on his way with the help of their 'good hands' (line 10) and 'gentle breath' (line 11).
- He hopes that the audience will forgive any faults in the play they have just seen.

WHY IS THIS SCENE IMPORTANT

A **Prospero** speaks directly to the **audience** with **humility**.

B With this final speech, Prospero's life on the **island**, his **magic** powers and the **play** itself are brought to an **end**.

KEY THEME: POWER

There is a paradox in the play's epilogue as Prospero, finally returning to Milan after years of exile with his dukedom again in safe hands, speaks about his powers declining. Not only has he set aside his magical powers but he also appears to be concerned about the effects of getting older. In Act IV Scene 1 he refers to his 'old brain' (line 159) and his 'infirmity' (line 160) and in Act V Scene 1 he explains that he will 'retire me to Milan, where/Every third thought shall be my grave' (line 311–12). Now that Prospero's important work is complete, Shakespeare reveals to the audience a frailer Prospero whose thoughts begin to move towards his own death.

KEY CONTEXT (A03)

The Tempest is generally considered to be Shakespeare's final play – though he did go on to write three more works with John Fletcher.

AIMING HIGH: SHAKESPEARE'S FINAL WORDS ⭐

Make sure you also consider the dramatic importance of the epilogue. Shakespeare is showing the audience that since the play has reached its end, the power of the actors to entertain will soon cease. Throughout the epilogue, he asserts the audience's power to judge the performance and, effectively, to set the actors free. Prospero hopes that the audience will use their 'good hands' (line 10) to 'release me from my bands' (line 9) by applauding the performance. Similarly the audience's 'gentle breath' (line 11) can be interpreted as verbal thanks and praise for the performance they have just watched and heard. To what extent do you think we should view this epilogue as a comment by Shakespeare about his own artistic powers?

PROGRESS AND REVISION CHECK

SECTION ONE: CHECK YOUR KNOWLEDGE

1 Who usurped Prospero's title and lands?

2 What is the name of Alonso's kingdom?

3 What does Miranda say she remembers from before she came to the island?

4 Whose kindness does Prospero remember in Act I Scene 2?

5 Which three physical objects are associated with Prospero's magic powers?

6 Who stays on board the supposedly shipwrecked vessel?

7 Who is the first noble character to leap into the sea?

8 Where is the rest of the king's fleet?

9 Who was brought to the island pregnant long before the actions of the play begin?

10 Where was Ariel imprisoned for twelve years?

11 What does Prospero accuse Ferdinand of in Act I Scene 2?

12 How is Claribel related to characters in the play?

13 What does Antonio encourage Sebastian to do in Act II Scene 1?

14 What are Stephano and Trinculo's occupations?

15 Which two characters hide under a cloak in Act II Scene 2?

16 Who does Stephano say would be his queen?

17 What mysteriously appears and disappears in Act III Scene 3?

18 What is used as a lure to catch Stephano, Trinculo and Caliban in the act of stealing?

19 Which game are Miranda and Ferdinand playing in the final scene of the play?

20 Who brings Alonso the news that his ship is unscathed and seaworthy?

PROGRESS AND REVISION CHECK

SECTION TWO: CHECK YOUR UNDERSTANDING

Here are two tasks about the significance of particular moments in the play. These require more thought and slightly longer responses. In each case, try to write at least three to four paragraphs:

Task 1: Look again at Act I Scene 1. What is significant about this scene in relation to the rest of the play? Think about:

- The importance of the events that are taking place in this scene
- What we learn about some of the play's main characters

Task 2: Comment on the importance of the conversation that takes place between Antonio and Sebastian in Act II Scene 1 lines 197–296. Think about:

- What is being discussed and planned
- Parallels and contrasts with other parts of the play

PROGRESS CHECK

GOOD PROGRESS

I can:

- understand how Shakespeare has sequenced and revealed events. ☐
- refer to the importance of key events in the play. ☐
- select well-chosen evidence, including key quotations, to support my ideas. ☐

EXCELLENT PROGRESS

I can:

- refer in depth to main and minor events and how they contribute to the development of the plot. ☐
- understand how Shakespeare has carefully ordered or revealed events for particular effects. ☐
- draw on a range of carefully selected key evidence, including quotations, to support my ideas. ☐

WHO'S WHO?

Alonso
King of Naples

Sebastian
brother of Alonso

Prospero
magician and rightful
Duke of Milan

Antonio
brother of Prospero
and usurping Duke of Milan

Ferdinand
son of Alonso

Miranda
daughter of Prospero

Ariel
spirit and servant of Prospero

Adrian, Francisco
and other courtiers

Gonzalo
honest councillor

Caliban
Prospero's slave
and son of Sycorax

Trinculo
jester

Stephano
butler

Boatswain, Master
and ship's crew

PROSPERO

PROSPERO'S ROLE IN THE PLAY

Prospero was the Duke of Milan until his brother Antonio overthrew him and cast him and his daughter adrift at sea. During the play:

- he is a dutiful and loving father to Miranda who was banished with him.
- he commands Ariel and other spirits to perform magical tasks according to his wishes.
- he keeps Caliban as his slave on the island.
- he creates the storm that causes Alonso and his companions to reach the island.
- he arranges the meeting of Ferdinand and Miranda who fall in love.
- he eventually reunites King Alonso of Naples with Ferdinand, his son and heir.
- he forgives those who wronged him and renounces his magic powers before returning to Milan.

PROSPERO'S IMPORTANCE TO THE PLAY AS A WHOLE

KEY CONTEXT (A03)

Famous alchemists included the Swiss physician Paracelsus (1493–1541) and the English mathematician and astrologer John Dee (1527–1608) who was also known for having the largest private library in England at that time.

Prospero's ambition to return home with his daughter and claim their birthright provides the play with its central story. Prospero's powers are so extensive that, much like an author, he influences everything that occurs in *The Tempest* from the storm at the beginning to granting Ariel his freedom at the end.

AIMING HIGH: MAGIC AND ALCHEMY ⭐

The very best answers will make interesting connections between characters, themes and relevant contextual information. In *The Tempest*, Prospero refers in a variety of ways to his plan to be reinstated as the Duke of Milan and at the beginning of Act V Scene 1 he says 'Now does my project gather to a head' (line 1). He is associated from the beginning of the play with a love of books and study, and it is clear from the first scene in which he appears that he possesses magic powers. Many aspects of Prospero's behaviour and appearance would have put Shakespeare's audiences in mind of alchemy – a medieval philosophy concerned with transforming base metals into gold and discovering the elixir of life.

Alchemists were sometimes accused of dabbling in witchcraft and occultism. Shakespeare takes care to portray Prospero as a very different kind of practitioner to the 'damned witch Sycorax' (I.2.263). Furthermore, having recovered his earthly powers he relinquishes his magic, thereby demonstrating that he is motivated by justice rather than by greed. Ironically, Prospero's books are both the cause of his downfall and the means by which he takes back control.

EXAM FOCUS: WRITING ABOUT PROSPERO (A01)

Key point	Evidence/Further meaning
• Prospero is a bookish and learned man with an interest in the 'liberal arts' (I.2.73).	• He became so absorbed in his 'secret studies' (I.2.77) that his brother Antonio was able to become more involved in governing Milan and to eventually plot his overthrow.
• He is an attentive father to Miranda and takes great care that she receives an excellent education on the island.	• He insists that Miranda was not a 'trouble' (I.2.51) to him but 'a cherubin … that did preserve me' (lines 152–3). • He refers to himself as Miranda's 'schoolmaster' (line 172) and says he has 'made thee more profit/Than other princes can' (lines 172–3).
• He can be stern and severe in his dealings with others.	• In Act I Scene 2 he calls Ariel 'moody' (line 244) and 'malignant' (line 257) and calls Caliban 'malice' (line 367) and 'poisonous slave' (line 319). • Miranda says that Prospero is 'of a better nature … Than he appears by speech' (I.2.496–7). However Ferdinand believes him to be 'composed of harshness' (III.1.9).
• Ultimately he shows forgiveness to those who conspired against him.	• In Act V Scene 1, he says that 'The rarer action is/In virtue than in vengeance' (lines 27–8) before instructing Ariel to release the wrongdoers and bring them to him.

REVISION FOCUS: WRITING ABOUT PROSPERO

Throughout the play, Prospero's powers are in evidence even when he is not. Make notes on Prospero's hidden role in the play's nine scenes. In which scenes does he affect events without appearing at all? In which scenes is he unseen and unheard by the other characters on stage with him? How does this affect and shape the audience's response to him as the play progresses?

TOP TIP (A02)

In Latin, the word *prospero* means 'favourable' or 'prospering', suggesting that the fortunes of Shakespeare's central character will improve over the course of the play.

KEY CONTEXT (A03)

In the 2010 film version of *The Tempest* Helen Mirren is cast in the play's central role and is renamed Prospera. What effect might this have on the story?

MIRANDA

MIRANDA'S ROLE IN THE PLAY

Miranda is the fourteen- or fifteen-year-old daughter of Prospero. During the play:

- she cannot remember her previous life in Milan and has lived all of her life since then on the island.
- she has had no experience of human society beyond her father and is astonished when she meets first Ferdinand and, later on, the other noblemen from the ship.
- she falls in love with Ferdinand and agrees to marry him.
- we see that she has educated by Prospero in ways in which an aristocratic young woman should behave.
- she is nervous around Caliban because he has attempted to assault her, even though she taught him how to speak.
- she is welcomed into the Neapolitan royal family by a delighted Alonso.

EXAM FOCUS: WRITING ABOUT MIRANDA **A01**

Key point	Evidence/Further meaning
• Miranda's first words in the play establish her compassionate nature.	• In Act I Scene 2, Miranda says 'I have suffered/With those that I saw suffer' (lines 5–6). • Later in the play, she attempts to assist Ferdinand in his labours: 'I'll bear your logs the while' (III.1.24).
• She is instantly physically attracted to Ferdinand and wishes to be married to him.	• She says in Act I Scene 2 that 'There's nothing ill can dwell in such a temple' (line 457). • She finds it difficult to hide her feelings in Act III Scene 1: 'I am your wife, if you will marry me' (line 83).

TOP TIP: FERTILITY AND SUCCESSION **A01**

As well as being an important character in her own right, Miranda is also important as a symbol of order and succession. By marrying Ferdinand and bearing children, she provides assurance that Prospero's descendants will also govern Milan. The play contains several references to fertility and reproduction. In Act III Scene 1, Miranda uses pregnancy as a metaphor to describe her desire: 'The bigger bulk it shows' (line 81). The masque in Act IV Scene 1 also celebrates fertility and reproduction but Prospero insists that the young lovers must 'not give dalliance/Too much the rein' (lines 51–2) at the beginning of the scene, perhaps suggesting that he is anxious to ensure their children will be legitimate heirs.

ARIEL

ARIEL'S ROLE IN THE PLAY

Ariel is a magical, musical spirit who carries out a series of tasks for his master in the hope of achieving his freedom. During the play:

- he reports to Prospero that he has created the storm at sea just as instructed, magically preserving the ship and ensuring everyone survives.
- he is responsible for ensuring Ferdinand comes ashore separately from his father and noble shipmates, and leads him to Prospero and, crucially, to Miranda.
- he saves Alonso and Gonzalo from an assassination attempt.
- he appears playing the goddess Ceres in the masque Prospero arranges for Miranda and Ferdinand.
- he lures Stephano, Trinculo and Caliban to Prospero's cell where they are caught stealing.
- he brings Alonso, Antonio and Sebastian to be judged and eventually pardoned for their crimes towards Prospero.

EXAM FOCUS: WRITING ABOUT ARIEL
(A01)

Key point	Evidence/Further meaning
● Ariel appears eager to please Prospero who frequently praises his work.	● The first time he appears, he calls Prospero 'great master' and says he comes 'To answer thy best pleasure' (I.2.189–90). ● Prospero's praise for Ariel can be very tenderly expressed, for example 'Bravely the figure of the harpy hast thou/Performed, my Ariel; a grace it had, devouring' (III.3.83–4).
● As Prospero's servant, Ariel is always busy – but he craves his freedom from Prospero.	● Ariel is portrayed as having great energy and vitality and he sometimes shows his mischievous side, for example when he teases Trinculo by imitating his voice in Act III Scene 2. ● Ariel demands his 'liberty' in Act I Scene 2 line 245 and he is excited in Act V Scene 1 at the imminent prospect of being granted his freedom.
● Although he is a spirit, Ariel understands human nature and is capable of kind and compassionate feelings towards people.	● Prospero is touched that Ariel 'which art but air' (line 2) feels moved by the imprisoned men's wretched state in Act V Scene 1.

CALIBAN

CALIBAN'S ROLE IN THE PLAY

Caliban, the son of the witch Sycorax, is Prospero's slave. He has lived on the island longer than any other character. During the play:

- he claims that the island is his and that Prospero repaid his kindness in showing him the island by enslaving him.
- he is resentful of the work he must do for Prospero but, though he complains and curses, he is fearful of his master and does what he is told.
- he meets Trinculo and Stephano and starts to believe that Stephano is a godlike figure who could be his new master.
- He and Trinculo plot against Prospero but are unsuccessful.
- he may or may not remain on the island at the end.

EXAM FOCUS: WRITING ABOUT CALIBAN   (A01)

Key point	Evidence/Further meaning
• Caliban has an extensive knowledge of the island and which he generously shares with newcomers.	• He showed Prospero the island when he first arrived: 'And then I loved thee,/And showed thee al the qualities o'th'isle' (I.2.36–7). • He also offers to show Stephano and Trinculo the island's riches in Act II Scene 2.
• Caliban's appearance startles and confuses people.	• Miranda says in Act I Scene 2 that he is 'a villain, sir,/I do not love to look on' (lines 309–10). • Stephano and Trinculo refer to him as a 'mooncalf' (II.2.111) and a 'monster' (III.2.25). • Alonso says he 'is a strange thing as e'er I looked on' (V.1.290).
• He can be angry, resentful and rebellious, fearful and cowering	• Caliban curses and complains about Prospero his master in Act I Scene 2: 'The red plague rid you' (line 364). • In Act I Scene 2 Caliban acknowledges that he 'must obey' Prospero because 'His art is of such power' (line 372).

KEY QUOTATION: 'KING' CALIBAN   (A01)

In Act I Scene 2 lines 341–2 Caliban states: 'For I am all the subjects that you have,/Which first was mine own king'. He is pointing out the reversal that has taken place in his fortunes, from being 'king' of the island to being Prospero's slave.

ANTONIO

ANTONIO'S ROLE IN THE PLAY

Antonio is Prospero's usurping younger brother and the current Duke of Milan. During the play:

- he appears in the storm scene and blames the boatswain and crew for their predicament.
- he successfully persuades Sebastian to attempt to kill his brother Alonso, just as he deposed his own brother Prospero – but their attempts are thwarted.
- he is forgiven by Prospero but shows no sign of repenting – and it is Alonso who restores to Prospero his dukedom.

EXAM FOCUS: WRITING ABOUT ANTONIO (A01) ✎

Key point	Evidence/Further meaning
● Antonio betrays Prospero and usurps his dukedom and title.	● In Act I Scene 2 lines 68–9, Prospero says to Miranda that Antonio was 'next thyself,/Of all the world I loved' showing that he had placed a great deal of trust in his brother. ● Prospero also calls his brother 'perfidious' (line 68), meaning treacherous or disloyal.
● He makes some tactically clever political decisions.	● Antonio wins the support of Alonso, King of Naples – though Prospero considers this to be 'ignoble stooping' (I.2.116). ● Antonio also chose to remove Prospero and Miranda from Milan but does not damage his own reputation by having them killed.
● He is capable of drawing others into his conspiracies.	● Antonio's persuasive skills and understanding of the parallels between Sebastian's situation and his own lead him to successfully convince Sebastian to make an attempt on his brother's life.

KEY QUOTATION: PROSPERO'S VIEW (A01)

Antonio is the antagonist to Prospero's protagonist, a trusted brother who exploits and betrays that trust. It is useful to analyse Prospero's description of how his neglect of his worldly duties 'Awaked an evil nature' (I.2.93) in his brother and he uses the simile 'my trust,/Like a good parent, did beget of him/A falsehood' (lines 93–5) to describe the terrible consequences of his own inaction. Shakespeare uses personification here to describe trust as a well-meaning but naive 'good parent'.

ALONSO

ALONSO'S ROLE IN THE PLAY

Alonso is the King of Naples and father to Ferdinand and Claribel. During the play:

- we learn that he played a part in supporting Antonio's overthrow of Prospero and that he bears some of the responsibility for this injustice.
- his ship is caught in a storm on the return journey from his daughter Claribel's wedding in Tunis.
- he comes ashore with the other nobles but believes his son and heir Ferdinand has drowned.
- he is sorry for what he has done and asks for forgiveness.
- he is overjoyed to find his son is alive and engaged to Prospero's charming daughter Miranda.

EXAM FOCUS: WRITING ABOUT ALONSO (A01)

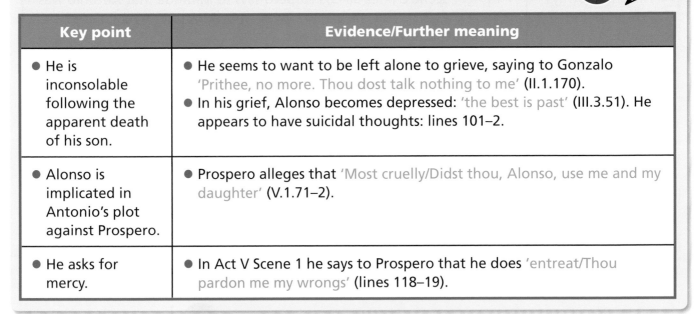

Key point	Evidence/Further meaning
• He is inconsolable following the apparent death of his son.	• He seems to want to be left alone to grieve, saying to Gonzalo 'Prithee, no more. Thou dost talk nothing to me' (II.1.170). • In his grief, Alonso becomes depressed: 'the best is past' (III.3.51). He appears to have suicidal thoughts: lines 101–2.
• Alonso is implicated in Antonio's plot against Prospero.	• Prospero alleges that 'Most cruelly/Didst thou, Alonso, use me and my daughter' (V.1.71–2).
• He asks for mercy.	• In Act V Scene 1 he says to Prospero that he does 'entreat/Thou pardon me my wrongs' (lines 118–19).

KEY CONTEXT (A03)

The name Alonso is the Spanish form of Alfonso. In the fifteenth century there were two kings of Naples with this name: Alfonso I and Alfonso II. Both kings had sons called Ferdinand.

TOP TIP: WRITING ABOUT ALONSO'S LANGUAGE (A02)

Alonso makes his presence in the play felt more as a father in mourning than as a powerful king. He does not take the lead in Act II Scene 1 as his men come to terms with their new island environment, preferring to be left to grieve. In Act III Scene 3 his thoughts become more morbid: 'the thunder,/That deep and dreadful organ-pipe' (lines 97–8) and 'deeper than e'er plummet sounded' (line 101). Shakespeare uses repetition to show that Alonso is increasingly preoccupied with his son's death – and with his own death too; 'I wish/Myself were mudded in that oozy bed/Where my son lies' (V.1.150–2) echoes almost exactly his words in Act III Scene 3 lines 100–2.

FERDINAND

FERDINAND'S ROLE IN THE PLAY

Ferdinand is the son and heir to King Alonso of Naples. During the play:

- he is the first to escape from the ship – he is separated from the other nobles and is brought to Prospero and Miranda by Ariel.
- he believes his father is drowned and that he may be the sole survivor of the shipwreck.
- he instantly falls in love with Miranda and vows he will make her 'the Queen of Naples' (I.2.149).
- he is accused by Prospero of being a 'traitor' (line 469) and an 'impostor' (I.2.477) and is given 'labours' (III.1.7) to perform such as gathering wood.
- he is shown to be truly in love with the 'perfect and peerless' Miranda (III.1.47).
- he is reunited with his father in the play's final scene and prepares to return to Naples with his bride.

EXAM FOCUS: WRITING ABOUT FERDINAND

Key point	Evidence/Further meaning
● He is greatly affected by the magic he witnesses.	● During the storm his hair is 'up-staring' (I.2.213) and he cries out 'Hell is empty/And all the devils are here!' (lines 214–15). ● He is delighted by the 'majestic vision' (IV.1.118) of the masque and asks 'May I be bold/To think these spirits?' (lines 119–20).
● His treatment of Miranda is courtly and chivalrous.	● For the sake of his beloved, he says he is prepared to endure hardship: 'for your sake/Am I this patient log-man' (III.1.66–7)
● He is a loving and loyal son.	● He mourns his father even as he ponders that he has inherited his crown: 'Myself am Naples,/Who with mine eyes, never since at ebb, beheld/The king my father wrecked' (II.1.434–6).

TOP TIP: THE EFFECTS OF ENCHANTMENT **A01**

Ferdinand's first appearance in the play is in Act I Scene I though the first lines we hear him speak are in Act I Scene 2 as Ariel draws him to Prospero and Miranda with an enchanting song. He asks questions – 'Where should this music be? I'th'air, or th'earth?' (line 387) – and describes Ariel's music as having a powerful effect: 'This music crept by me upon the waters,/Allaying both their fury and my passion/With its sweet air' (lines 391–3). He quickly understands that 'This is no mortal business' (line 406) and the audience begins to build an impression of him as someone who is sensitive and open to new experiences.

SEBASTIAN

SEBASTIAN'S ROLE IN THE PLAY

Sebastian is Alonso's younger brother and one of the shipwrecked nobles who also played a part in Prospero's downfall. During the play:

- he and Antonio curse the boatswain and mock Gonzalo.
- he blames his brother Alonso for the 'loss' (II.1.123) of both Claribel (through marriage) and Ferdinand (by drowning).
- he is easily persuaded by Antonio to attempt to assassinate his brother Alonso.
- he is forgiven by Prospero but shows no sign of repenting.

EXAM FOCUS: WRITING ABOUT SEBASTIAN (A01)

Key point	Evidence/Further meaning
● His language can be angry and abusive.	● In Act I Scene 1, he hurls insults at the boatswain: 'A pox o' your throat, you bawling, blasphemous, incharitable dog!' (line 40–1).
● He seems lazy and needs to be pushed into action.	● Sebastian's phrase 'Hereditary sloth' (II.1.222) refers to his inaction and perhaps also to an idle son who is not the heir.
● At the end of the play he does not repent.	● When Prospero accuses Sebastian of being 'a furtherer in the act' (V.1.73) and a traitor, Sebastian accuses him of being possessed by the devil: 'The devil speaks in him!' (line 129).

AIMING HIGH: CRITICISING THE KING

In Act II Scene 1, Sebastian blames his brother King Alonso both for the loss of Alonso's daughter from the royal courts of Europe (because she has married an African king), and for the loss of his son whom they suppose has drowned on the return journey from Claribel's wedding. His language is extremely direct: 'you may thank yourself for this great loss' (line 123) and 'The fault's your own' (line 135). Afterwards, Gonzalo suggests to Sebastian that his language 'doth lack some gentleness' (line 137). Consider how the actor playing Sebastian might deliver these lines. He could be feeling frustrated with his brother and speaking with emotion, or it might be a more calculated attempt to undermine and provoke his brother.

GONZALO

GONZALO'S ROLE IN THE PLAY

Gonzalo is an honest and kind Neapolitan councillor who comes ashore with Antonio, Alonso, Sebastian and the other courtiers after the storm. During the play:

- we learn that Gonzalo took pity on Prospero and Miranda and brought them provisions to aid their survival as well as Prospero's beloved books.
- he tries to lift King Alonso's spirits when they come ashore, but to no avail, and is mocked by Sebastian and Antonio for doing so.
- he speaks about the kind of ideal society he would create on the island.
- his life is in danger when Antonio and Sebastian are plotting to kill the king.
- he joyfully summarises all the ways in which the play has ended happily.

EXAM FOCUS: WRITING ABOUT GONZALO

Key point	Evidence/Further meaning
• Gonzalo is a kind-hearted and generous man.	• In Act I Scene 2, Prospero refers to his 'charity' (line 162). • He tries to be open-minded and see behind appearances, saying in Act III Scene 3 'there are people of the island –/Who, though they are of monstrous shape, yet note/Their manners are more gentle, kind, than of/Our human generation' (lines 30–3).
• He readily shares his advice and observations with others.	• He finds the boatswain impertinent and advises him to 'remember whom thou hast aboard' (I.1.19). • He speaks at length about the kind of society he would wish for 'had I plantation of this isle' (II.1.143).
• His outlook on life is generally optimistic.	• In Act II Scene 1 he advises the king to be positive and 'weigh,/Our sorrow with our comfort' (lines 8–9).

TOP TIP: WRITING ABOUT GONZALO

As well as considering what characters say in the play, you can also analyse the comments other characters say to and about them. For example, Antonio and Sebastian mock Gonzalo in Act II Scene 1: 'Look, he's winding up the/watch of his wit. By and by it will strike' (lines 14–15). These comments seem cruel, but do have an element of truth in them as they draw attention to Gonzalo's tendency to be talkative, fussy and perhaps a little unrealistic at times. However, Gonzalo is also given high praise by Prospero who commends his loyalty (lines 68–70).

STEPHANO AND TRINCULO

STEPHANO AND TRINCULO'S ROLES IN THE PLAY

Stephano (a butler) and Trinculo (a jester) are returning to Naples with the king when their ship is caught in the storm. During the play:

● they are reunited after the storm and discover Caliban.

● together with Caliban, who hopes to have found a new master in Stephano, they plot to kill Prospero.

● they are lured by Ariel to Prospero's cell and are chased away by spirits in the shape of dogs and hounds.

● Prospero returns them to King Alonso.

EXAM FOCUS: WRITING ABOUT STEPHANO AND TRINCULO (A01)

Key point	Evidence/Further meaning
● Caliban starts treating Stephano like his master, and Trinculo mocks him.	● In Act II Scene 2, Caliban says 'I will kiss thy foot. I prithee, be my god' (lines 148–9). ● Trinculo mutters 'When god's asleep, he'll rob his bottle' (line 151).
● They are frequently drunk and disorderly.	● When Stephano first appears in Act II Scene 2, he is 'singing, with a bottle'. ● Act III Scene 2 opens with a disagreement about drinking: 'Tell not me! When the butt is out we will drink water, not a drop before' (lines 1–2). ● Ariel describes them as 'red-hot with drinking' (IV.1.171).
● They are undone by their greed.	● Stephano is tempted in Act III Scene 2 by the idea of being 'king' of the island (line 108). ● In Act IV Scene 1, Stephano and Trinculo are distracted from their murder plot by the trinkets and clothing they have found.

TOP TIP (A01)

Stephano and Trinculo's are comic characters. Make notes about what makes their scenes particularly humorous, and consider how these comic elements could be brought out in the actors' performances.

AIMING HIGH: EVERYDAY ENGLISH

You will gain more marks if you can make perceptive comments about the variety of language used by Shakespeare and the effects of his language choices. The dialogue spoken by Stephano and Trinculo is largely written in prose to denote the characters' lower status and comic function. Much of the language Shakespeare gives them is close to vernacular English (everyday language) and includes expressions such as 'Thy eyes are almost set in thy head' (III.2.8–9), which is slang for 'You're drunk'. Elsewhere Shakespeare uses well-known proverbs and sayings for example when Stephano says to Caliban 'Here is that which will give language to you, cat' (II.2.82–3), he is alluding to the proverb 'Ale will make a cat speak'.

MINOR CHARACTERS

THE SHIP'S MASTER, THE BOATSWAIN AND THE SHIP'S CREW

The master, boatswain and crew of the ship appear in Act I Scene 1, when the ship is battling the storm. The master and boatswain reappear in Act V Scene 1 to report the ship's miraculously seaworthy condition following the tempest. These characters perform a number of other functions, providing a glimpse into the lives of characters from other classes and backgrounds; they remind the audience that sea voyages require the efforts of many different people. This is the first of several moments in the play when Shakespeare seems to encourage the audience to reflect on human society and on how much importance we attach to rank and status.

ADRIAN, FRANCISCO AND THE OTHER COURTIERS

Among King Alonso's 'train' (V.1.301) are the lords Adrian and Francisco and an unspecified number of other courtiers. They are also victims of the storm and come ashore after leaving the ship. Both Adrian and Francisco appear to be helpful and loyal men, having more in common with Gonzalo than with Antonio and Sebastian. In Act II Scene 1, Adrian tries to find positive things to say about the island and is mocked, along with Gonzalo. Francisco tries to reassure the king that his son 'may live' (line 113) but Alonso is sure that 'he's gone' (line 122). In Act III Scene 3, Adrian and others 'of suppler joints' (line 107) are enlisted by Gonzalo to come to the aid of Alonso, Antonio and Sebastian.

KEY CONTEXT (A03)

Some of the characters in *The Tempest* appear to have been inspired by commedia del'arte, a theatrical form that began in Italy in the sixteenth century. Character types included elderly masters, young lovers and devious servants.

KEY QUOTATION: FRANCISCO'S REPORT (A02)

Francisco, one of the lords travelling with Alonso, speaks only twice in the whole play. However his relatively lengthy speech in Act II Scene 1 is important because he gives an eyewitness report of Prince Ferdinand coming ashore. Even though King Alonso does not believe this piece of good news, the audience knows it to be true, having seen Ferdinand in the previous scene. Francisco's tone shows respect and admiration for the man of whom he speaks: 'his bold head' (line 117), 'good arms' and 'lusty stroke' (line 119). Although we know that Ferdinand's fate is ultimately in Prospero's hands, Shakespeare is also showing us that Ferdinand possesses strengths and qualities that make him a promising heir to Alonso's crown.

UNSEEN FEMALE CHARACTERS

A number of important characters are mentioned but do not appear in the play. Caliban's mother Sycorax was a powerful witch who was brought to the island after being banished from Algiers. Prospero mentions in Act I Scene 2 that she died without releasing Ariel from his imprisonment. We are also told about Alonso's daughter and Ferdinand's sister, the *'fair'* Claribel (II.1.72) who has married the King of Tunis. Alonso is returning from her wedding when his ship is caught in a storm. There is also a brief mention of Miranda's mother who died, we are led to assume, when Miranda was very young.

TOP TIP (A01)

It's helpful to think about the different ways in which authority is challenged in the play, from the boatswain's supposed impudence in giving orders to his important passengers, to Antonio's usurpation of Prospero.

PROSPERO'S SPIRITS

In *The Tempest,* Prospero's *'art'* (I.2.1) gives him authority over the island's spirits. Not only does the *'airy spirit'* Ariel carry out instructions on behalf of his master, but numerous other spirits also play parts in Prospero's interventions. In Act III Scene 3, for example, the spirits play the parts of *'strange shapes'* and in Act IV Scene 1 *'divers Spirits in shape of dogs and hounds'* appear. Prospero explains to Ferdinand during the masque earlier in this scene that the players in the masque are *'Spirits, which by mine art/I have from their confines called to enact/ My present fancies'* (lines 120–2). We are reminded in this scene of qualities that would have been associated with magical spirits in the imaginations of Shakespeare's audiences: Prospero says the *'spell is marred'* (line 127) unless there is silence, and he describes the spirits' capacity to melt *'into thin air'* (line 150), a reference to the popular belief that spirits only became visible when the air from which they are formed thickened.

REVISION FOCUS: LEARN KEY QUOTATIONS

It is vital to support all your points about *The Tempest* with quotations. You will need to be ready to write about any of the characters that appear in the play.
Short quotations that you can embed within a sentence are of particular use when you are writing in timed conditions. Challenge yourself to select quotations of no more than eight words spoken by or about each character and record them on individual character pages within your notes. Look back at them often and aim to learn them by heart.

PROGRESS AND REVISION CHECK

SECTION ONE: CHECK YOUR KNOWLEDGE

1. About whom does Gonzalo say 'his complexion is perfect gallows'?

2. How are Prospero and Antonio related?

3. Who is described as a 'blue-eyed hag'?

4. How old is Miranda?

5. Who is mocked by Sebastian and Antonio in Act II Scene 1?

6. Who says that he witnessed Ferdinand swimming ashore from the storm?

7. Which character is grief-stricken for most of the play?

8. Who thinks he has found a creature with four legs and two mouths?

9. What are the names of the three classical goddesses who appear in the masque?

10. Who says that Miranda 'will outstrip all praise/And make it halt behind her'?

> **TOP TIP** (A01)
>
> Answer these quick questions to test your basic knowledge of the novel's characters.

SECTION TWO: CHECK YOUR UNDERSTANDING

Task: To what extent would you describe Shakespeare's portrayal of Caliban as sympathetic?

Consider:

- how Caliban speaks about his own situation;
- how he is spoken about and treated by others.

> **TOP TIP** (A01)
>
> This task requires more thought and a slightly longer response. Try to write at least three to four paragraphs.

PROGRESS CHECK

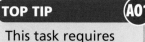

GOOD PROGRESS

I can:

- explain the significance of the main characters in how the action develops. ☐
- refer to how they are described by Shakespeare and how this affects the way we see them. ☐

EXCELLENT PROGRESS

I can:

- analyse in detail how Shakespeare has shaped and developed characters over the course of the play. ☐
- infer key ideas, themes and issues from the ways characters and relationships are presented by Shakespeare. ☐

THEMES

THEME TRACKER (A01)

Political power

● Act I Scene 2 lines 75–6: Prospero suggests he let his brother become too involved in affairs of state.

● Act II Scene 1 lines 206–8: Antonio urges Sebastian to grasp the opportunity to become king.

● Act V Scene 1: Ferdinand and Miranda's chess game **foreshadows** their return to Naples as future heads of state.

POLITICAL POWER

Many different types of power are at work in *The Tempest*, both human and supernatural. Shakespeare gives us a fascinating insight into the workings of political power in his account of how Prospero lost his dukedom and in his portrayal of the scheming Antonio:

● Prospero explains to Miranda in Act I Scene 2 the circumstances by which he was overthrown as Milan's head of state. He reflects on the factors that led to his downfall, particularly his own fondness for study rather than government and Antonio's 'ambition' (line 105) and 'foul play' (line 62).

● He acknowledges his brother's political skills – 'Being once perfected how to grant suits [favours]/How to deny them, who t'advance, and who/To trash for over-topping' (lines 79–81) – and success in winning the hearts and minds of the people and in 'stooping' (line 116) to the King of Naples to win his favour. He also describes how Antonio's growing ambition made him self-deceiving and increasingly obsessed with power: 'Made such a sinner of his memory/To credit his own lie' (lines 101–2). Antonio's determination to convince Sebastian to oust King Alonso – 'What a sleep were this/For your advancement!' (II.1.267–8) – gives the impression of a man who is greedy for ever more influence.

● Antonio is seen to act unjustly, but he is nonetheless a fascinating portrayal of a cunning and ruthless political operator. We may draw a parallel between his approach to winning and maintaining power with the principles advocated by Niccolò Machiavelli in *The Prince* (1513).

KEY CONTEXT (A03)

In the fourteenth century Italy was comprised of various states of great importance. Milan, Naples, Florence, Venice and the Papal States were all independently ruled.

⭐ AIMING HIGH: SHAKESPEARE AND THE CYCLE OF POWER

The very best answers will show excellent understanding of relevant concepts in their discussion of key themes. For example, political power games, succession and usurpation are ideas Shakespeare returns to again and again in his plays.

Many of Shakespeare's plays depict power struggles and violent usurpations. These include the history plays such as *Richard II* in which the king is overthrown by Henry Bolingbroke and *Henry IV Part 1* in which Bolingbroke (now King Henry) has to defend his crown against a challenger. Shakespeare's most famous tragedies including *Macbeth* and *Hamlet* also show power changing hands by means of treachery and violence. By watching these plays, the audience explores the minds and motivations of rulers and their rivals and witnesses the toppling of powerful figures as time passes and fortune's wheel turns.

KEY QUOTATION: FAIR AND FOUL · **A01**

In *The Tempest,* Antonio is careful not to be seen to harm his victims. Miranda asks 'Wherefore did they not/That hour destroy us?' (I.2.138–9). Prospero replies that they did not dare to because of 'the love my people bore me' (I.2.141). The circumstances of the father and daughter's removal from Milan show that Antonio does not want to stain his reputation by being seen as a murderer. In this way, Antonio and his ministers, to use Prospero's striking **metaphor**, 'With colours fairer painted their foul ends' (I.2.143). The language

here implies that Antonio understands the importance of how his behaviour is viewed and interpreted by the people. His instinct to control his image in the public eye – to make a 'foul' injustice appear 'fairer' than it should – is a further example of his political skill.

REVENGE AND FORGIVENESS

Throughout the play there are many mentions of violent punishments and threats of revenge, but also moments of forgiveness:

- Sycorax inflicted a terrible 'torment' on Ariel, and Caliban lists numerous ways in which Prospero could be violently murdered.

- As the play reaches its climax, it seems that it might end in Prospero taking revenge on those who have treated him so poorly. However, Prospero ultimately chooses 'virtue' over 'vengeance'.

- The mood at the end of the play is generally harmonious and forgiving. Gonzalo lists all the happy outcomes that have been achieved 'in one voyage', Prospero welcomes all the characters to his 'poor cell', and an engagement is celebrated.

- However, not all the characters share Prospero's forgiving attitude at the end of the play. Alonso is sorrowful and wishes to be pardoned but Antonio and Sebastian do not seek forgiveness.

REVISION FOCUS: CALIBAN

You could compare some of the different ways in which the role of Caliban has been interpreted. Is he a beast or a man? Is an evil character or a victim of the colonial greed of 'civilised' men? Is his desire for revenge on Prospero justified?

THEME TRACKER **A01**

Revenge and forgiveness

- Act III Scene 2 lines 53–5: Caliban encourages Stephano to help him get his revenge on Prospero.

- Act IV Scene 1 lines 192–3: Prospero says that he will 'plague' Caliban, Stephano and Trinculo for plotting against him.

- Act V Scene 1 lines 25–8: Prospero is forgiving even though he has been 'struck to th' quick' by 'high wrongs'.

THEME TRACKER (A01)

Magic

- Act I Scene 2 lines 1–2: Miranda refers to her father's magic powers or 'art' in raising the storm.
- Act IV Scene 1: Prospero tells Ferdinand the masque was an illusion acted by spirits.
- Act V Scene 1 lines 50–1: Prospero announces 'But this rough magic/I here abjure'.

MAGIC

From the sea-storm in Act I Scene 1 onwards, we see and hear evidence of Prospero's magic powers:

- Three **symbolic** items represent Prospero's powers: his 'magic garment' (I.2.24), his 'book' (III.1.94) and his 'staff' (V.1.54). In Act V Scene 1, he takes care not only to renounce his magical powers but also to 'bury' (line 55) and 'drown' (line 57) these items so that they cannot fall into the wrong hands.
- Throughout the play Prospero is able to summon and command Ariel and the other spirits to do his work. By these means, Shakespeare shows us that Prospero is fully in control of his magic powers, rather than being controlled by them.
- We can draw a parallel between Prospero and the 'foul witch Sycorax' (I.2.258) who was also aided 'by help of her more potent ministers' (line 275) from the spirit world. But Prospero's account tells us that she 'could not again undo' (line 291) her imprisonment of Ariel and that only Prospero's 'art' (line 291) could free him. He also suggests that Sycorax used her magic callously, 'in her most unmitigable rage', and disproportionately, for Ariel's punishment was 'a torment/To lay upon the damned' (lines 289–90).
- Sycorax's magic is presented as evil. She was banished 'For mischiefs manifold, and sorceries terrible' (line 264), though it is important to remember that we only have Prospero's account of the story to go on.

THEME TRACKER (A01)

Freedom and servitude

- Act I Scene 2 line 245: Ariel demands 'my liberty'.
- Act II Scene 2 lines 180–6: Caliban celebrates his new master with 'Freedom, high-day!'
- Act V Scene 1 lines 88–94: Ariel sings in anticipation of his hard-won freedom.

FREEDOM AND SERVITUDE

Prospero's relationships with his servant, the spirit Ariel, and particularly with his slave Caliban may seem harsh and even cruel by contrast with his other relationships in *The Tempest*.

- Ariel's service to Prospero takes the form of a series of magical tasks that Ariel must perform to win his freedom.
- When challenged about the terms of their agreement, Prospero reminds Ariel that he freed him from his long imprisonment at the hands of Sycorax, before threatening to imprison him once more 'If thou more murmur'st' (I.2.294).
- Meanwhile Caliban is repeatedly referred to as a slave and in this capacity he carries out lowly tasks for his master such as collecting wood and washing dishes.
- Caliban's speeches in the play contain complaints about how he suffers at the hands of Prospero's other spirits, angry curses and bitter criticism of his master.
- Generally, however, both Ariel and Caliban are obedient to their master because, as Caliban puts it, 'His art is of such power' (line 372).
- At the end of the play Prospero honours his promise to Ariel: 'Then to the elements/Be free, and fare thou well' (V.1.318–19). Whether freedom is a genuine prospect for Caliban is a matter for debate:
- Shakespeare leaves his fate unresolved at the end of the play and it is unclear whether he would remain on the island after Prospero and Miranda leave for Naples.

THEATRE AND SPECTACLE

The Tempest contains many performances:

- Ariel is often involved in performances as he carries out the magical tasks Prospero has assigned to him. Some of these performances are truly spectacular in nature, such as when Ariel addresses Alonso, Antonio and Sebastian dressed as a harpy in Act III Scene 3, the masque in Act IV Scene 1, or the sea-storm with which the play begins.
- These scenes, with their cast of spirits and intriguingly described special effects, would have made full use of the Elizabethan/Jacobean stage and the latest stagecraft techniques.
- There are also enchanting musical performances; indeed Ariel's entrances are usually accompanied by music. These performances further the action of the play and contribute to its mood and effects on the audience who – like the characters – may feel entertained, moved and puzzled by what they have seen and heard.

There are also some more direct references to theatre in the play:

- In Act III Scene 3, Sebastian likens the vision he has witnessed to 'A living drollery' (line 21) or puppet show with living players.
- In Act IV Scene 1 the impermanence and artificiality of theatrical effects are likened to the shortness of life itself.
- In the play's epilogue, Prospero addresses the audience directly yet humbly, describing the hold the audience has over the actors as a 'spell' (line 8).
- In what was to be one of Shakespeare's final works for the stage, the playwright celebrates the gorgeous but brief 'vision' (IV.1.51) that is theatre.

THEME TRACKER A01

Theatre and spectacle

- Act III Scene 3: Alonso and his fellow travellers witness a strange spectacle.
- Act IV Scene 1 lines 151–6: Prospero comments on the transience of theatre and of life.
- Epilogue lines 9–13: Prospero hopes for the audience's appreciation at the end of the play.

THEME TRACKER (A01)

Learning and education

● Act I Scene 2 lines 171–5: Prospero proudly describes how he tutored Miranda and she thanks him.

● Act I Scene 2 lines 363–5: Caliban rebukes Miranda and Prospero for 'learning me your language'.

● Act IV Scene 1 lines 188–92: Prospero regrets that his attempts to educate and improve Caliban have failed.

LEARNING AND EDUCATION

One of the first things the audience learns about Prospero in *The Tempest* is his love of books and learning.

● In his account of how Antonio took his dukedom, Prospero explains that he was so 'transported/And rapt in secret studies' (I.2.76–7) that he neglected 'worldly ends' (line 89). By devoting himself to the 'bettering of his mind', he left himself vulnerable to his brother's plotting.

● Prospero believes in the importance of education, becoming a 'careful' (line 174) tutor to his daughter Miranda and instilling in her that same conviction about its value.

● We learn that Miranda 'took pains' (line 354) to teach Caliban language but both she and Prospero note with regret that their efforts have been insufficient to alter what they view as Caliban's true nature: 'A devil, a born devil,' says Prospero in Act IV Scene 1, 'on whose nature/Nurture can never stick' (lines 188–9). Shakespeare seems to be suggesting here and elsewhere that education and upbringing or 'nurture' have their limitations.

TOP TIP (A01)

Prospero's plans depend on Ferdinand and Miranda falling in love. How does Prospero create opportunities for Ferdinand and Miranda to meet and for their love to develop?

REVISION FOCUS: LOVE

Don't forget that other more minor themes have a role to play. For example, Prospero's plans depend on Ferdinand and Miranda falling in love. How does Prospero create opportunities for Ferdinand and Miranda to meet and for their love to develop? Make a list, and look for other examples of love in the play.

CONTEXTS

SHAKESPEARE'S LATER YEARS

William Shakespeare (1564–1616) was a popular playwright in his lifetime and a favourite of both Elizabeth I and then James I, who allowed Shakespeare's theatre company the great honour of being called the King's Men. *The Tempest* was written and first performed on 1 November 1611 at court. It is generally considered to be Shakespeare's last play that wasn't written in collaboration with another writer. The play has many similarities with Shakespeare's other late plays: the use of the romance genre, the freedom with which Shakespeare uses iambic pentameter, his tendency to use fewer rhyming couplets and more blank verse as his writing style developed.

The Tempest is generally held to be the work of an extraordinary writer at the height of his powers. Some critics have poignantly observed that in it, the playwright is perhaps reflecting on age and the prospect of his artistic and physical powers diminishing, particularly in the character of Prospero. Shakespeare was also commenting and reflecting on events at the time of writing. The play was performed in the winter of 1612/13 in celebration of the marriage of the king's daughter Elizabeth to the elector of Palatine, Prince Frederick V. The elaborate festivities planned by King James included a fireworks display, a mock sea-battle, masques, banquets and pageantry. It seems likely that Shakespeare intended that his audience draw a parallel between the two 'masters of ceremonies': King James and Prospero.

JACOBEAN DRAMA

Drama continued to flourish under King James I (see picture) with William Shakespeare and Ben Jonson (1572–1637) the most popular playwrights of the time. Among his many achievements, Jonson contributed greatly to the development of both the masque and the anti-masque, and is seen to have been an influence on Shakespeare's masque in Act IV Scene 1 of *The Tempest*. Another popular style of drama at this time was the revenge play, of which John Webster's *The Duchess of Malfi* (1613) is perhaps the most well-known example today.

KEY CONTEXT (A03)

Ben Jonson's masques written for King James' court include *The Satyr* (1603) and *The Masque of Blackness* (1605). *The Satyr* features fairies and elves as well as classical figures. *The Masque of Blackness* opens with a spectacular sea-storm created by billowing cloths.

CLASSICAL MYTHS AND LEGENDS

The Tempest contains many allusions to classical myths and legends. Many educated theatre-goers would have been familiar with famous passages from them in the original Latin or in the popular English translations.

AENEAS AND THE HARPIES

The *Aeneid* is an epic poem by the Roman poet Virgil (70BC–19BC). It tells the story of the Trojan hero Aeneas whose long travels after the Trojan War take him from Troy to Italy via many Mediterranean locations. These locations include Carthage where Aeneas has an affair with Queen Dido, to whom Shakespeare refers in Act II Scene 2. The journey Alonso and the others take as they return to Italy from Claribel's wedding in Tunisia carries echoes of some of the locations and journeys in Virgil's poem. In Act III Scene 3, Shakespeare alludes to an episode in the *Aeneid* in which Aeneas and his men arrive at the Strophades islands in the Ionian Sea where harpies (see **Part Four: Contexts – Classical Myths and Legends**) take their food from them and tell Aeneas he must travel on to Italy.

MEDEA THE SORCERESS

Prospero's speech that begins 'Ye elves of hills, brooks, standing lakes, and groves' (V.1.33) draws extensively on a passage by another Roman poet Ovid (43BC–AD17/18). In his book *Metamorphoses*, Ovid writes about transformations of men, women or gods into animals in Greek and Roman mythology, and in Book VII he writes about the magician Medea who uses her magic to bring a character back to life – much as Prospero will appear to do when he reunites Alonso and Ferdinand. However Medea is a vengeful figure, unlike Prospero, whose thoughts at this point in the play are of forgiveness.

TRAVELS TO DISTANT LANDS

Shakespeare was writing at a time when European explorers continued attempts to sail around the globe and discover 'new' places. They also had ambitions to take over these places and make them part of their empires – a process known as colonisation. Ideas of travel, exploration and colonisation are in evidence throughout the play:

- Caliban describes in Act I Scene 2 how he welcomed the newcomer Prospero to his island home 'And showed thee all the qualities o'th'isle' (line 337) but feels his goodwill was exploited.
- In Act II Scene 1 lines 143–68, Gonzalo imagines how he would create an ideal society on the island.
- In Act II Scene 2, Stephano imagines offering a tamed Caliban as a gift from his travels: 'he's a present for any emperor' (lines 69–70).
- In Act III Scene 3 lines 1–10, Alonso, Gonzalo and the others feel lost and downhearted as they explore the island.
- In Act III Scene 3, Alonso and the others are so amazed by what they have seen and heard that they say they are now inclined to believe even the more far-fetched tales of travellers.

KEY CONTEXT (A03)

It has been suggested that the events in the play might have been inspired by the real-life survival story of how the ship *Sea Venture* survived a storm off the coast of Bermuda (see **Part Two: Act I Scene 1 – Key context**).

SETTINGS

A STORM AT SEA

- The action of *The Tempest* takes place on an enchanted island with the exception of the first scene, which takes place on board Alonso's ship during the sea-storm.
- Shakespeare uses nautical words and phrases in this scene, for example when the boatswain says 'Lay her a-hold, a-hold! Set her two courses off to sea again, lay her off!' (I.1.48–9). The boatswain's urgent commands to the others convey the danger of the situation in which the ship's crew and passengers find themselves, as do the numerous references to sinking, drowning and death.

THE ENCHANTED ISLAND

- Shakespeare leaves much scope to the imagination in his description of the island, and directors and set designers through the centuries have imagined it in a host of different ways.
- Some details of the remote island are given. Ariel describes the 'odd angle of the isle' (I.2.223) where Ferdinand comes ashore and the 'deep nook' (line 227) that provides a natural harbour for the king's ship.
- We learn something of the landscape of the island: its 'hard rock' (line 343), trees including 'pine' (line 277), 'oak' (line 294) and lime ('the line-grove' – V.1.10) and its other flora and fauna (see **Part Five: Motifs – Flora and Fauna**).
- In Act II Scene 1, Gonzalo and Adrian describe the island to King Alonso: 'How lush and lusty the grass looks! How green!' (line 55), 'The air breathes upon us here most sweetly' (line 49), though their remarks are made more to lift Alonso's spirits than to give an accurate description of the landscape.
- Sebastian and Antonio provide a contrasting view, describing the ground as 'tawny' (line 56) and the air 'as 'twere perfumed by a fen' (line 51). After spending some hours on the mysterious island, it still feels like a 'maze' (line 2) to the men marooned on it as they follow its 'forthrights and meanders' (line 3).

PROSPERO'S CELL

- When Ariel leads Stephano, Trinculo and Caliban to Prospero's dwelling, he takes them through 'Toothed briars, sharp furzes, pricking gorse, and thorns' (IV.1.180) and into 'th'filthy-mantled pool beyond your cell' (line 182).
- The word 'cell' (1.2.20) alludes to a monk's room and brings with it connotations of humility and simple religious living. Shakespeare helps the reader to imagine the lowliness of Prospero's dwelling and the inhospitable nature of the island that has been home to a duke in exile and his daughter for twelve years.

TOP TIP (A01)

The 1623 first folio of the *The Tempest* describes the play's 'scene' or location as 'an uninhabited island'. No exact location of the island is given in the play.

KEY CONTEXT (A03)

The island is a strange mix of British (bogs, thistles) and exotic (lush grass, herds of lions) flora and fauna.

PROGRESS AND REVISION CHECK

SECTION ONE: CHECK YOUR KNOWLEDGE

1 Why is Tunis important in the play?

2 Who calls Caliban 'Abhorred slave' in Act I Scene 2?

3 Who does Antonio say 'ne'er did lie, /Though fools at home condemn 'em' (III.3.26–7)?

4 To whom does Antonio say that he can see 'a crown/Dropping upon thy head' in Act II Scene 1?

5 At what time of day are we told Prospero and Miranda were forced to leave Milan?

6 What is the 'vanity of mine art' (line 41) that Prospero arranges for Ferdinand and Miranda in Act IV Scene 1?

7 With what kind of ceremony is the Greek god Hymen associated?

8 What does Adrian mean when he describes the island as 'desert' (line 37) in Act II Scene 1?

9 Which place is described as the 'salt deep' in Act I Scene 2 and as 'that oozy bed where my son lies' in Act V Scene 1?

10 Who describes himself as 'master of a full poor cell' (I.2.20)?

> **TOP TIP**   **A01**
>
> Answer these quick questions to test your basic knowledge of the themes, contexts and settings of the play.

SECTION TWO: CHECK YOUR UNDERSTANDING

Explain how Shakespeare explores the themes of learning and education in *The Tempest*.

Think about:

- the importance of learning and education in the play.
- how different attitudes to these themes are presented.

> **TOP TIP**   **A01**
>
> This task requires more thought and a slightly longer response. Try to write at least three to four paragraphs.

PROGRESS CHECK

GOOD PROGRESS

I can:

- explain the main themes, contexts and settings in the text and how they contribute to the effect on the reader.   ☐
- use a range of appropriate evidence to support any points I make about these elements.   ☐

EXCELLENT PROGRESS

I can:

- analyse in detail the way themes are developed and presented across the play.   ☐
- refer closely to key aspects of context and setting and the implications they have for the writer's viewpoint, and the interpretation of relationships and ideas.   ☐

FORM

OVERVIEW

Many of Shakespeare's plays can be classified into one of three genres: comedies, tragedies or histories. However *The Tempest* is one of several plays that are more difficult to classify.

IS IT A COMEDY?

The play shares some key features with comedies; it ends happily for its central characters Prospero and Miranda with a wedding and their safe return to the Italian setting of Milan. Many of the characters are also typical of comedy: Miranda the beautiful and virtuous maid, Ferdinand her princely suitor, Gonzalo the loyal friend. From the lower classes, Stephano and Trinculo provide humorous interludes to the main action and their underhand antics are only mildly troubling to the others. At the end, forgiveness holds sway and harmony is restored.

OR A ROMANCE?

However, the word romance (or late romance) is more commonly used to describe *The Tempest* and several of Shakespeare's other late plays including *The Winter's Tale* and *Cymbeline.* A romance can be defined as a fiction set in a distant time and place featuring unusual events and characters. The play's strange and supernatural content, its disorientating setting and the loneliness and suffering described (albeit much of this is in the past before the action of the play itself has begun) make *The Tempest* an intriguing and highly original work of literature.

KEY CONTEXT (A03)

Many songs and speeches from the *The Tempest* have become famous as songs and lyric poems in their own right, and the play has been an inspiration to artists across many media including poetry, art and music. Sir Kenneth Branagh performed Caliban's speech 'Be not afeard, the isle is full of noises' at Danny Boyle's opening ceremony of the 2012 Olympic Games.

TOP TIP: MASQUES AND SONGS (A01)

Shakespeare includes a masque in Act IV Scene 1 (see **Part Two: Plot and action – key form: Masque**). *The Tempest* features more music than any other play by Shakespeare, and contains several songs. Many are sung by Ariel and they play an important part in conjuring for the audience the strange sounds and magical atmosphere of the island. Ariel's songs are in themselves magical, achieving powerful effects on their listeners. For example, Ferdinand says of Ariel's song beginning 'Come unto these yellow sands' that he did not follow the music as such, rather 'it hath drawn me' (I.2.394). By way of contrast, the play also includes Stephano's rowdy sea shanties in Act II Scene 2 and Act III Scene 2's tuneless 'Flout 'em and scout 'em' (line 122). Make sure you can write about the effect of the masques and songs.

STRUCTURE

OVERVIEW

The Tempest is one of Shakespeare's shortest plays and has only nine scenes. Its action is continuous and effectively takes place in real time, with Shakespeare making several references to the fact that only a few hours have passed since the storm. For example, in the final scene, when the boatswain mentions 'three glasses' (line 223) he means three hours (the word 'glass' meaning hourglass) referring to his use of an hourglass to measure time.

THE STORM SCENE

This nautical scene – the only scene in The *Tempest* not set on the island – serves as a kind of introduction to the main events of the play. It is action-packed and depicts an event so significant that it sets in motion everything that follows. Shakespeare uses the scene to establish the theme of power and to introduce us to key characters in the play's central power struggle.

RECOUNTING THE PAST

In Act 1 Scene 2 several stories are recounted that describe events that took place before the action of the play began. First Prospero tells Miranda how his brother Antonio usurped his position as Duke of Milan and sent the two of them into exile twelve years ago. Going further back in time, Shakespeare also provides details of Ariel and Caliban's back stories both in their own words and in Prospero's version of events. The audience also learns about the witch Sycorax who was banished from her home in Algiers and arrived on the island pregnant with Caliban.

THE EPILOGUE

An epilogue comes at the end of a piece of writing and can be described as a final comment by the author. *The Tempest* concludes with an epilogue of twenty lines delivered by Prospero. In this epilogue, Prospero speaks both of the fictional world of the island from which he is about to set sail and of the theatre in which his performance is nearing its conclusion. The use of shorter line length and rhyming couplets in the epilogue help to make this passage of verse sound different to what has preceded it, and bring closure to the play (see **Part Two: Epilogue summary**).

KEY CONTEXT (A03)

In his book *Poetics*, the Greek philosopher Aristotle suggests that plays should obey three rules: unity of action, unity of time and unity of place. With its lack of subplots, short time frame and single location on the island, *The Tempest* comes closer to Aristotle's ideal than many of Shakespeare's other plays.

LANGUAGE

OVERVIEW

Shakespeare's language in *The Tempest* is often described using words like 'dreamlike', 'musical' and 'poetic'. The playwright uses a range of techniques to create a variety of striking effects:

- Shakespeare's inventive choice of words, use of certain motifs and powerful imagery are among the play's most celebrated features.
- The language of the play is rich in contrasts; we find elevated formal verse and vernacular prose, prayers and curses, elegant expressions of love and violent expressions of hatred.
- It is also a play in which language, like music, is written about as having a particular power – from Prospero's attachment to his library to the discussion of the 'profit' to Caliban of 'learning me your language!' (I.2.365).

LANGUAGE DEVICE: SOUND EFFECTS

What are sound effects?	Sound effects are how words sound when spoken aloud and how these sounds correspond to the words' meaning. They include alliteration, assonance, onomatopoeia and rhyme.
Example	'I flamed amazement …The fire and cracks/Of sulphurous roaring the most mighty Neptune/ Seem to besiege' (Ariel, 1.2.198–205).
Effect	The assonant long vowel sounds of 'flamed amazement' and 'seem to besiege' along with the onomatopoeia of 'cracks' and 'roaring' evoke the sounds of fire and the speed and power with which fire spreads. 'Most mighty' refers to the power of another deadly element with which the fire appears to be warring: the sea.

REVISION FOCUS: REPETITION

Make notes in your text about the use of repetition within individual speeches in the play. Compare the effects of repetition in different kinds of speech, for example, in curses and insults, in grand speeches and incantations, and in more private and personal words of love and loss. How does this language analysis support your deeper understanding of character and motivation?

TOP TIP (A02)

A line of iambic pentameter generally has ten syllables, but Shakespeare varies the syllable count in his plays to achieve different effects. Many lines in *The Tempest* have feminine endings, that is to say they end on an unstressed eleventh syllable. Find examples of this and write about what you feel the effect is (for example, gentle, magical).

LANGUAGE DEVICE: IMAGERY

What is imagery?	Imagery is vivid and descriptive language that helps the reader to understand and respond to what a character says.
Example	'she that from whom/We were all sea-swallowed, though some cast again' (II.1.249–50).
Effect	The sea is described here as having first swallowed the ship's passengers and then vomited them back up again. This description of the passengers being thrown into the sea and then washed up on the island shore is an example of both metaphor and personification as the sea is described as having human characteristics.

KEY QUOTATION: ANALYSING ARIEL'S SONG (A01)

'Full fathom five thy father lies' is a short rhyming 'ditty' (I.2.405) with deeper meanings for its listener Ferdinand because it refers to his father Alonso and the likelihood that he has drowned and lies on the seabed. Ariel uses powerful and haunting imagery – 'Those are pearls that were his eyes./Nothing of him that doth fade/But doth suffer a sea-change' (I.2.398–400) – but ends the song with his customary childlike rhymes and repetitions – 'Sea-nymphs hourly ring his knell. Hark, now I hear them, ding dong bell' (lines 403–4). Despite the funereal word 'knell', Shakespeare's language in this song does not dwell entirely on death but on the possibility of 'change'. This could be seen to foreshadow Alonso's penitence at the end of the play.

TOP TIP (A03)

You could make notes about Shakespeare's use of rhyming couplets and tetrameter in the epilogue and what you think the effects of these language choices on the audience might be.

LANGUAGE DEVICE: COMPOUND WORDS

What are compound words?	Compound words are two words linked together with a hyphen to create a new meaning.
Examples	'The elements/… may as well/Wound the loud winds, or with bemocked-at stabs/Kill the still-closing waters' (III.3.61–4).
Effect	Ariel's use of compound words in this speech adds to the speech's intensity and makes the judgement passed on the three 'men of sin' all the more forceful.

LANGUAGE DEVICE: MOTIFS

What are motifs?	Motifs are images that are repeated throughout the play and acquire a particular significance.
Example	<ul><li>'there they hoist us/To cry to th'sea that roared to us' (I.2.148–9)</li><li>'I shall no more to sea, to sea/Here shall I die ashore' (II.2.42–3)</li><li>'the sea mocks/Our frustrate search on land' (III.3.9–10)</li></ul>
Effect	The frequent references to the sea in the play have a cumulative effect on the listener and serve to remind the characters and the audience of the power of the sea, both to destroy and to transport.

FLORA AND FAUNA

Nature provides other recurring motifs in the play:

- Caliban is shown to have knowledge of the island's natural environment and how to survive on its 'crabs', 'pignuts', 'filberts' and 'scamels' (II.2.167–72). The earthy sounds of these words help to connect Caliban to the earth and to the pursuits of foraging and scavenging.

- Imagery from nature such as 'she did litter here/A freckled whelp' (I.2. 282–3) and 'A strange fish!' (II.2.27) are used by characters to attempt to describe Caliban's unusual physical appearance.

- The nobles' uncertainty about what kinds of creatures might exist on the island makes them uneasy and they become scared at the thought of 'bulls, or rather lions' (II.1.312) roaming about.

- The natural world is also presented as a hostile environment when a variety of creatures such as 'apes' (line 9), 'hedgehogs' (line 10) and 'adders' (line 13) appear in Caliban's description of how Prospero's spirits punish him in Act II Scene 2.

SUFFERING, PUNISHMENT AND VIOLENCE

- Before the play began, Ariel suffered imprisonment in a tree 'where thou didst vent thy groans/As fast as millwheels strike' (I.2.280–1).

- Caliban complains that Prospero's spirits torment him with pinches, bites and taunts. In turn, Caliban's curses and plots – 'Batter his skull, or paunch him with a stake,/Or cut his weasand with thy knife' (III.2.91–2) – are violent and sadistic.

- Prospero uses vengeful language in the play – 'I will plague them all' (IV.1.192) – although he ultimately forgives those who wronged him.

PROGRESS AND REVISION CHECK

SECTION ONE: CHECK YOUR KNOWLEDGE

1. In which scene does the tempest occur?

2. Complete this rhyming couplet Ariel sings: 'Full fathom five, thy father lies,/Of his bones are coral made;'

3. Who delivers the play's epilogue?

4. Which character is mentioned but not by name?

5. In which scene does Prospero stage a masque and why?

6. How many syllables can you count in this line of verse: 'With eyes wide open – standing, speaking, moving' (II.1.213)?

7. Which word in these lines spoken by Prospero is a compound word: 'How to deny them, who t'advance, and who/To trash for over-topping' (I.2.80–1)?

8. Which word in this line spoken by Gonzalo is an example of onomatopoeia: 'Upon mine honour, sir, I heard a humming' (II.1.317)?

9. Which of these words spoken by Ariel is a simile: 'So I charmed their ears/That calf-like they my lowing followed' (IV.1.178–9)?

10. Which language device does Shakespeare use in the phrase 'Twelve year since, Miranda, twelve year since' (I.2.53)?

TOP TIP (A01)

Answer these quick questions to test your basic knowledge of the form, structure and language of the novel.

SECTION TWO: CHECK YOUR UNDERSTANDING

How does Shakespeare use language to convey feelings of romantic love?

Think about:

- Miranda and Ferdinand's relationship and engagement;
- the language and imagery Shakespeare uses.

TOP TIP (A02)

This task requires more thought and a slightly longer response. Try to write at least three to four paragraphs.

PROGRESS CHECK

GOOD PROGRESS

I can:

- explain how Shakespeare uses form, structure and language to develop the action, show relationships and develop ideas. ☐
- use relevant quotations to support the points I make, and make reference to the effect of some language choices. ☐

EXCELLENT PROGRESS

I can:

- analyse in detail Shakespeare's use of form, structure and language to convey ideas, create characters and evoke mood or setting. ☐
- select from a range of evidence, including quotations, to talk about the effect of particular language choices and to develop wider interpretations. ☐

PART SIX: PROGRESS BOOSTER

UNDERSTANDING THE QUESTION

For your exam, you will be answering an extract-based question and/or a question on the whole of *The Tempest*. Check with your teacher to see what sort of question you are doing. Whatever the task, questions in exams will need **decoding**. This means highlighting and understanding the key words so that the answer you write is relevant.

TOP TIP (A01)

You may not have time to write such a detailed plan in the exam, but this is a good example of how to structure your ideas into paragraphs. Remember to back up your points with evidence from the text, events or quotations.

BREAK DOWN THE QUESTION

Pick out the **key words** or phrases. For example:

Read the text from Act I Scene 2 line 237 ('Ariel, thy charge/Exactly is performed') to line 304 ('Hence with diligence').

Question: How does Shakespeare **present attitudes** towards **freedom and servitude** in **this extract** and in the **play as a whole**?

What does this tell you?

- Focus on the **themes of freedom and servitude** but also on **different characters'** views on them.
- The word **'present'** tells you that you should focus on the ways Shakespeare reveals these attitudes – the techniques he uses.
- The phrases **'this extract'** and **'play as a whole'** mean you need to **start** with the given **extract** and then **widen your discussion** to the rest of the play, but sticking to the theme **in both**.

PLANNING YOUR ANSWER

It is vital that you generate ideas quickly and plan your answer efficiently when you sit the exam. Stick to your plan and, with a watch at your side, tick off each part as you progress.

TOP TIP (A04)

Remember that spelling, punctuation and grammar are worth **approximately 5%** of your overall marks, which could mean the difference between one grade and another.

STAGE 1: GENERATE IDEAS QUICKLY

Briefly **list your key ideas** based on the question you have **decoded**. For example:

- In the **extract** Ariel insists that Prospero promised him his freedom.
- Prospero presents himself as Ariel's saviour because he rescued him from the tree in which Sycorax had imprisoned him, but threatens further imprisonment if Ariel does not follow his instructions.
- In the **play as a whole** Caliban is also critical of Prospero's treatment of him and he begins to follow and serve Stephano.
- Caliban believes he has found freedom when he has merely become another man's servant.
- Gonzalo is a loyal servant of Prospero.

STAGE 2: JOT DOWN USEFUL QUOTATIONS (OR KEY EVENTS)

For example, from the **extract**:

'Dost thou forget/From what a torment I did free thee?' (lines 250–1)

From the **play** as a whole:

Act II Scene 2, 'I'll kiss thy foot. I'll swear myself thy subject' (line 152)

STAGE 3: PLAN FOR PARAGRAPHS

Use paragraphs to plan your answer. For example:

Paragraph	Point
Paragraph 1	**Introduce** the **argument** you wish to make: *In this extract, Shakespeare presents differing attitudes to being a servant or a slave. At the beginning of the extract, Ariel is impatient to be given his freedom as he was promised but this contrasts with the end in which he accepts that he must continue to work for Prospero or face the consequences.*
Paragraph 2	Your first point: *Ariel addresses Prospero directly and freely: 'Let me remember thee what thou hast promised.' He is asserting his right to be free and believes he is entitled to this because he has worked hard for Prospero.*
Paragraph 3	Your second point: *Prospero reminds Ariel that he freed him from the tree in which Sycorax imprisoned him for twelve years. In this way, Prospero presents Ariel's service for him as a relative freedom, compared with the 'torment' he previously endured.*
Paragraph 4	Your third point: *Similarly, in Act II Scene 2, Caliban views working for a different master as a freedom of sorts and sings about the prospect of no longer having to work for Prospero. However his new master is little more than a drunken fool.*
Paragraph 5	Your fourth point: *Shakespeare shows the reader that fear is a key factor in keeping Ariel and Caliban in Prospero's service. Caliban does briefly plot against him, but his efforts are in vain and he seeks Prospero's 'grace' once more, just as Ariel sought Prospero's favour in Act I Scene 2 by meekly asking 'What shall I do?'*
Conclusion	**Sum up** your argument: *Shakespeare presents a range of attitudes towards servitude and slavery in the play ranging from accepting one's situation to rebelling against one's master. He also shows that both Caliban and Ariel dream – and sing – about the idea of winning their freedom.*

TOP TIP (A02)

When discussing Shakespeare's language, make sure you refer to the techniques he uses and, most importantly, the *effect* of those techniques. Don't just say, 'Shakespeare uses lots of insults and curses; write, 'Shakespeare's use of insults and curses shows/ demonstrates/ conveys the ideas that ...'

RESPONDING TO WRITERS' EFFECTS

The two most important assessment objectives are **AO1** and **AO2**. They are about *what* writers do (the choices they make, and the effects these create), *what* your ideas are (your analysis and interpretation) and *how* you write about them (how well you explain your ideas).

ASSESSMENT OBJECTIVE 1

What does it say?	What does it mean?	Dos and Don'ts
Read, understand and respond to texts. Students should be able to: ● Maintain a critical style and develop an informed personal response. ● Use textual references, including quotations, to support and illustrate interpretations.	You must: ● Use some of the literary terms you have learned (correctly!). ● Write in a professional way (not a sloppy, chatty way). ● Show that you have thought for yourself. ● Back up your ideas with examples.	**Don't write:** *Antonio is a very unkind brother who went behind his brother's back to become duke.* **Do write:** *Shakespeare presents Antonio as a ruthless and 'false' character, both in Prospero's account of how he was undermined and then 'hurried … aboard a barque' with his daughter in Act I Scene 2 and in the scenes in which Antonio himself appears.*

IMPROVING YOUR CRITICAL STYLE

Use a variety of words and phrases to show effects:

Shakespeare *suggests ..., conveys ..., implies ..., presents how ..., explores ..., demonstrates ..., describes how ..., shows how ...*

I/we (as readers) *infer ..., recognise ..., understand ..., question ..., see ..., are given ..., reflect ...*

For example, look at these two alternative paragraphs by different students about Gonzalo. Note the difference in the quality of expression.

Student A:

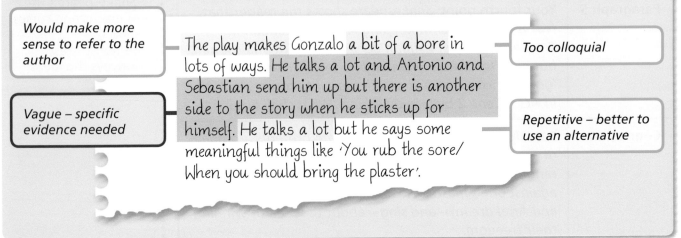

Would make more sense to refer to the author

Vague – specific evidence needed

The play makes Gonzalo a bit of a bore in lots of ways. He talks a lot and Antonio and Sebastian send him up but there is another side to the story when he sticks up for himself. He talks a lot but he says some meaningful things like 'You rub the sore/ When you should bring the plaster'.

Too colloquial

Repetitive – better to use an alternative

Student B:

Fits with the idea of the overall way Gonzalo is shown	*Clear and precise language*
Good variety of vocabulary	*Clear and precise language*

Shakespeare portrays Gonzalo as a talkative and perhaps overly attentive figure when he tries to comfort Alonso in Act II Scene I. However we also acknowledge his humanity and intelligence as he speaks sympathetically to the king and at length about his ideal society. His use of words like 'innocent', 'abundance' and 'perfection' convey not only his utopian ideals but also his positive view of the human race.

Looks beyond the obvious and infers meaning with personal interpretation

ASSESSMENT OBJECTIVE 2   (A02)

What does it say?	What does it mean?	Dos and Don'ts
Analyse the language, form and structure used by the writer to create meanings and effects, using relevant subject terminology where appropriate.	'Analyse' – comment **in detail** on **particular aspects** of the text or language. 'Language' – vocabulary, imagery, sound effects, rhythm and metre, etc. 'Form' – **how** the story is told (e.g. comedy or romance, five-act play, inclusion of a masque). 'Structure' – the **order** in which events are revealed, or in which characters appear, or descriptions are presented. 'Create meaning' – what can we, as readers, **infer** from what the writer tells us? What is **implied** by particular descriptions, or events? 'Subject terminology' – **words** you should use when writing about plays, such as 'audience', 'drama', 'act', 'scene', 'stage direction', etc.	**Don't write:** *The language helps the reader to understand that the island is a magical place.* **Do write:** *In this speech, Caliban's lyrical language has a peaceful and musical quality. Shakespeare uses onomatopoeia to convey the sounds of the 'twangling instruments'. The repetition of 'sleep'/'sleeping' gives a sense of being in a state halfway between sleeping and waking, trying to return to a beautiful dream.*

IMPLICATIONS, INFERENCES AND INTERPRETATIONS

- The best analysis focuses on specific ideas or events, or uses of language and thinks about what is **implied**.
- This means drawing **inferences**. From the beginning, Miranda is shown to be a kind and intelligent woman but what deeper ideas are signified in her language and in the language used about her?
- From the inferences you make across the text as a whole, you can arrive at your own **interpretation** – a sense of the bigger picture, a wider evaluation of a character, relationship or idea.

USING QUOTATIONS

One of the secrets of success in writing exam essays is to use quotations **effectively**. There are four basic principles:

1. Only quote what is most useful. Do not use a quotation that repeats what you have just written.

3. Put quotation marks, i.e. '...', around the quotation.

4. Write the quotation exactly as it appears in the original.

5. Use the quotation so that it fits neatly into your sentence.

EXAM FOCUS: USING QUOTATIONS

Quotations should be used to develop the line of thought in your essay, and to 'zoom in' on key details, such as language choices. The **mid-level response** below shows a clear and effective way of doing this:

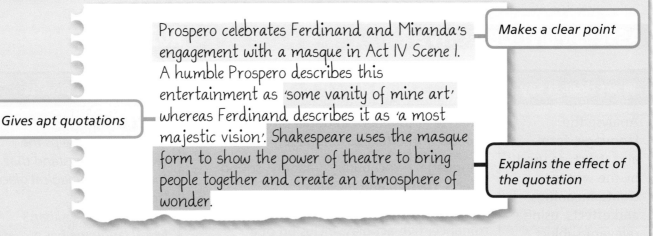

Prospero celebrates Ferdinand and Miranda's engagement with a masque in Act IV Scene I. A humble Prospero describes this entertainment as 'some vanity of mine art' whereas Ferdinand describes it as 'a most majestic vision'. Shakespeare uses the masque form to show the power of theatre to bring people together and create an atmosphere of wonder.

- Makes a clear point
- Gives apt quotations
- Explains the effect of the quotation

However, **High-level responses** will go even further. They will make an even more precise point, support it with an even more appropriate quotation, focus in on particular words or phrases, and explain the effect or what is implied to make a wider point or draw inferences. Here is an example:

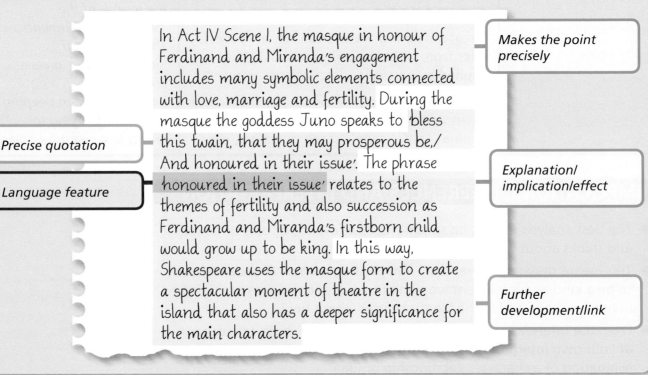

In Act IV Scene I, the masque in honour of Ferdinand and Miranda's engagement includes many symbolic elements connected with love, marriage and fertility. During the masque the goddess Juno speaks to 'bless this twain, that they may prosperous be,/ And honoured in their issue'. The phrase 'honoured in their issue' relates to the themes of fertility and also succession as Ferdinand and Miranda's firstborn child would grow up to be king. In this way, Shakespeare uses the masque form to create a spectacular moment of theatre in the island that also has a deeper significance for the main characters.

- Makes the point precisely
- Precise quotation
- Language feature
- Explanation/ implication/effect
- Further development/link

SPELLING, PUNCTUATION AND GRAMMAR

SPELLING

Remember to spell correctly the **author's** name, the names of all the **characters** and the names of **places**.

PUNCTUATION

Remember:

- Use **full stops and commas in sentences accurately** to make clear points. Don't get caught between a long, rambling sentence that doesn't make sense, and a lot of short repetitive ones. Write in a fluent way, using linking words and phrases.

Don't write	Do write
Ariel is associated with music throughout the play because Ariel sings songs and also music is usually playing when he comes on stage, and sometimes the other characters make comments about the beautiful strange music.	*Ariel is associated with music throughout the play. Shakespeare gives him a number of short rhyming songs to sing and his entrances are often accompanied by music.*

GRAMMAR

When you are writing about the text, make sure you:

- Use the present tense for discussing what the writer does.
- Use pronouns and references back to make your writing flow.

Don't write	Do write
In this scene, Antonio plotted with Sebastian the murder of Sebastian's brother King Alonso. In this way, Antonio hoped to increase Antonio's political power and influence in Naples as well as in Milan.	*In this scene, Antonio **plots** with Sebastian the murder of his friend's brother King Alonso. In this way, he **hopes** to increase his political power and influence in Naples as well as in Milan.*

TOP TIP (A04)

Practise the spellings of key literary terms you might use when writing about the text such as: allusion, metaphor, rhyming couplet, etc.

TOP TIP (A04)

Enliven your essay by varying the way your sentences begin. For example: *Prospero watches Ferdinand and Miranda to check on the progress of their relationship because he cannot make them fall in love* can also be written as: *Despite being able to contrive Ferdinand and Miranda's initial meeting, Prospero cannot make them fall in love.*

ANNOTATED SAMPLE ANSWERS

This section provides three sample responses, one at **mid** level, one at a **good** level and one at a **very high** level.

> **Question:** In Act IV Scene 1, Prospero 'starts suddenly and speaks' during the masque. Read from line 139 ('I had forgot that foul conspiracy') to line 193 ('Even to roaring').
>
> Starting with this extract, write about how Shakespeare presents Prospero's thoughts and feelings both here and in the play as a whole.
>
> Write about:
>
> - how Shakespeare presents Prospero's thoughts and feelings in this extract
> - how Shakespeare presents Prospero's thoughts and feelings elsewhere in the play

SAMPLE ANSWER 1

A02 Brief reference to a key form

In this extract, Prospero has just shown the masque to Miranda and Ferdinand for their engagement. It is as if he suddenly remembers ('I had forgot ...') that he has something very important to do and it is a matter of life and death because Stephano, Trinculo and Caliban have been plotting against him. He calls this plot 'a foul conspiracy' and he calls Stephano, Trinculo and Caliban 'confederates' and later on he calls them 'varlets' and 'thieves'. There are three of them which is like the other 'three men of sin' who plotted against Prospero.

A04 Too many clauses joined by 'and'

A01 Interesting link made

A01 Links to some key words from title about 'thoughts' and 'feelings'

Prospero is thinking that the performance must end and he must get back to his important work. But he seems to feel sad about the end of the 'revels' and he talks about this over quite a few lines showing that he is thinking deeply not just about the end of the play but the end of his time on the island and the fact that he is getting older as he talks about his 'old brain' and his 'infirmity'. So he is also talking about the end of his life.

From line 188, he seems to be very angry with Caliban. He is alone on stage when he says that 'Nurture can never stick' on Caliban. I think he feels he has tried with Caliban but

A01
Helpful example from elsewhere in play, but rather informal style

failed. This links with Act I Scene 2 when Prospero and Miranda let Caliban live with them and taught him to speak but they felt it was a failure.

A01
Clear point but does not add much to our overall understanding of Prospero

Then the scene shows that Prospero is still having to make plans and deal with things even now as he tells Ariel to get the 'trumpery', which are flashy clothes from his house, to catch Caliban and the others. So his work isn't done.

A01
Interesting discussion of key ideas from play

When Prospero says 'I will plague them all' he sounds like he wants his revenge on them. In actual fact he wants to frighten them but at the end of the play he learns that mercy and 'virtue' are more important than revenge. We know this because he says this to Ariel in Act V Scene I. He thinks that if Ariel can have pity on people and he is just a spirit, then he can feel pity too and forgive them.

A01
Short embedded quotations

So in this scene Prospero's thoughts and feelings are mixed and confused but he is working out what to do for the best. Shakespeare presents him as someone who is focused on what he needs to do but who still has worries and fears. He has magic powers but underneath it he also has 'my weakness'. This gets the audience's sympathy, a bit like in the epilogue where he says his powers are 'faint'. We get a feeling that his powers are slipping away.

MID LEVEL

Comment
Good points about Prospero are expressed about the extract and some relevant points are made about Prospero in other sections of the play. Some appropriate quotations are provided and there is some reference to the writer's purpose and effects.

For a Good Level:
- Develop a more fluent writing style.
- Make greater reference to the effects of language, structure and form with more references to Shakespeare.
- Provide more detailed explanations showing deeper understanding.
- Construct the argument more confidently.

SAMPLE ANSWER 2

A01
Helpful attempt to place extract in context

A04
Elegant expression of contrast

A02
Understanding of effects of literary technique

A02
Well expressed comment about a language technique and its effects

A01
Elegant and more conceptualised expression of ideas

A03
Point about context could be more closely linked to textual interpretation

A01
Clear reference to author's intentions

A04
Overuse of the word 'then'

A01
Fluent critical style

A04
Short sentences. It would be helpful to extend these ideas

In this scene, Prospero has just staged a masque for Ferdinand and Miranda. This was a popular entertainment in Shakespeare's time and included singing, dancing, dialogue and music. Suddenly there is a contrast with this mood of celebration and courtly entertainment as Prospero remembers there is something urgent he must attend to. His thoughts turn from 'my present fancies' to 'that foul conspiracy' and his feelings become very angry. Shakespeare emphasises this point by having Miranda say 'Never till this day/Saw I him touched with anger so distempered'.

However Prospero is strong and tries to hide his feelings. His first words are spoken in a private aside. Then he encourages Ferdinand to 'Be cheerful'. He then speaks at length about the end of the performance and he starts to use the idea that a theatrical performance is a metaphor for life. His imagery also suggests that the experience of watching a play is dreamlike. He uses many words like 'insubstantial' and 'baseless' which relate to the idea that there is something artificial about performance but also, in this case at least, something magical about it too. The actor spirits are capable of melting 'into thin air'.

By the end of this speech he is more upfront about his feelings saying things like 'Be not disturbed with my infirmity' and 'A turn or two I'll walk/To still my beating mind.' We are seeing a more vulnerable side to the mighty Prospero in this scene.

In the context of the rest of the play, this scene can perhaps be seen as a turning point as Prospero is very reflective and soul-searching, trying to work out what to do for the best. He seems to be very affected and frustrated by his failure to help Caliban. He thinks Caliban has resisted attempts to educate and civilise him. He says about Caliban that 'his body uglier grows' and 'his mind cankers'. Even though he is angry, he also seems concerned. Later in the scene he will say that he acknowledges that Caliban is 'mine'.

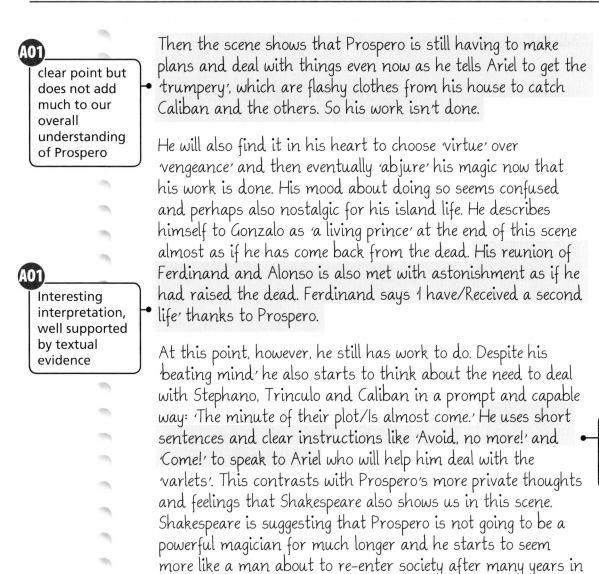

A01
clear point but does not add much to our overall understanding of Prospero

Then the scene shows that Prospero is still having to make plans and deal with things even now as he tells Ariel to get the 'trumpery', which are flashy clothes from his house to catch Caliban and the others. So his work isn't done.

He will also find it in his heart to choose 'virtue' over 'vengeance' and then eventually 'abjure' his magic now that his work is done. His mood about doing so seems confused and perhaps also nostalgic for his island life. He describes himself to Gonzalo as 'a living prince' at the end of this scene almost as if he has come back from the dead. His reunion of Ferdinand and Alonso is also met with astonishment as if he had raised the dead. Ferdinand says 'I have/Received a second life' thanks to Prospero.

A01
Interesting interpretation, well supported by textual evidence

At this point, however, he still has work to do. Despite his 'beating mind' he also starts to think about the need to deal with Stephano, Trinculo and Caliban in a prompt and capable way: 'The minute of their plot/Is almost come.' He uses short sentences and clear instructions like 'Avoid, no more!' and 'Come!' to speak to Ariel who will help him deal with the 'varlets'. This contrasts with Prospero's more private thoughts and feelings that Shakespeare also shows us in this scene. Shakespeare is suggesting that Prospero is not going to be a powerful magician for much longer and he starts to seem more like a man about to re-enter society after many years in exile.

A02
Understanding of language techniques and effects

GOOD LEVEL

Comment
The text is interpreted here thoughtfully in some detail and most points are supported by relevant evidence. There is some analysis of language and an attempt to understand the extract in the context of the scene from which it comes and in the context of the play, and of the character's development over the course of the play. The style of writing is fluent on the whole and there are the beginnings of an overall argument running through the answer.

For a High Level:
- Develop a coherent overall argument, expressed fluently and elegantly throughout.
- Make more links between close analysis and wider themes, effects of structure and form, etc.
- Demonstrate even more of a sense of the writer at work and analyse how effects are achieved.
- Ensure points about context are linked closely to the text and that they support textual interpretation.

SAMPLE ANSWER 3

A01 Powerful introduction of argument

In Prospero, Shakespeare has created a complex and sometimes paradoxical character: a master of magic who is also a disempowered duke, a kind father and teacher who also stands accused of being harsh and manipulative. He was ousted as Duke of Milan because he was too attached to his books but ironically it is through his learning that his fortunes now rise again. However, even though 'My charms crack not, my spirits obey', he does not feel triumphant as his plans near their end. Instead he is for the most part feeling anxious, thoughtful and even angry.

A01 Astute observations and well-chosen vocabulary

Shakespeare shows us in this scene that Prospero is anxious about the plot against his life and in general about getting older. He is on the verge of confronting those who have wronged him and of returning to his former life after twelve years on the island. In this time he has been able to use magic powers to summon spirits and make them do as he bids them and in this scene he is characteristically direct and firm with Ariel about what he has to do: 'We must prepare to meet with Caliban', 'Go bring it hither'. But he also speaks tenderly to Ariel calling him 'my bird' and praises him for charming the miscreants and leading them to the pool. It could be inferred from this tenderness that Prospero is beginning to feel sad that his magic is ending and that the airy spirit Ariel is about to be freed like a bird while he will return to more earthly concerns.

A01 Links ideas fluently

A01 Confident development of personal interpretation

His feelings about Caliban seem particularly complex. While he speaks about Caliban as one of the 'varlets', he also speaks privately about him in a more personal way that suggests he is disturbed by Caliban's failure to respond to the kindness he has been shown over the years. His phrase 'A devil, a born devil' seems to signal exasperation rather than ill-feeling. Indeed one might argue that he is genuinely concerned about what will become of Caliban and later in the scene he acknowledges that he is 'mine' and takes responsibility for him. However concerned he might be, it remains true that Prospero uses insulting words like 'beast' and 'bastard' to describe him unlike the newcomer Ferdinand who is already addressed with the familiar 'my son'.

A04 Short and direct topic sentence

A01 Effective choices of very short quotations

Prospero's long speech in this extract (lines 146-64) provides further insights into his mind at this turbulent time. He explains to Ferdinand and Miranda that the actors in the play were spirits who have now 'melted into air, into thin air'. Using impressive-sounding adjectives to enhance his description, he lists the grand buildings and thrilling vistas that a theatrical performance can present to an audience: 'the cloud-capped towers, the gorgeous palaces' in a highly rhetorical way, rather like an actor on a stage. Shakespeare is alluding to the power of theatre to create new worlds for example in masques which were very commonly associated with elaborate stage sets such as those Inigo Jones designed for Shakespeare's contemporary Ben Jonson.

A03 Relevant point about context

A02 Analysis of language choices and their effects and accurate use of literary terms

In turn, 'insubstantial pageant' becomes an extended metaphor for life itself: 'We are such stuff as dreams are made on'. Prospero's explanation to his young audience of how the joyful masque was staged becomes more reflective as he broods on the relative shortness of life and his own 'infirmity'. This awareness of his own mortality is also in evidence right at the end of the play when he says that when he retires to Milan 'Every third thought shall be my grave'. The reader can infer that returning to Milan is a new beginning for Miranda and Ferdinand but an ending for himself. It does at least seem, as his plans 'gather to a head' and the play reaches its climax, that the ending will be the one he has longed for, an ending he has strived throughout the play to achieve.

A04 Elegant sentence structure

VERY HIGH LEVEL

Comment
This answer provides a compelling exploration of text. The convincing argument is structured and expressed confidently, using detailed, focused analysis of language and comments about context that are relevant and which have been integrated well. The effect of the writer's choices is paramount in the extract and this is explored confidently and perceptively throughout. The writing style is elegant and fluent.

PRACTICE TASK

Write a full-length response to this exam-style question and then use the **Mark Scheme** on page 88 to assess your own response.

You can use the **General Skills** section of the **Mark Scheme** on page 88 to remind you of the key criteria you'll need to cover.

TOP TIP **A01**

Question: In Act I Scene 2, Prospero describes to Miranda how Antonio succeeded in usurping his title.

Read from line 53 ('Twelve year since, Miranda, twelve year since') to line 168 ('Would I might/But ever see that man').

Starting with this extract, how does Shakespeare present the themes of political power and ambition in this play?

Write about:

● how Shakespeare presents the themes of political power and ambition in this recounting of past events

● how Shakespeare presents the themes of political power and ambition in the play as a whole

Remember:

● Plan quickly and efficiently by using key words from the question.

● Write equally about the extract and the rest of the play.

● Focus on the techniques Shakespeare uses and the effect of these on the reader.

● Support your ideas with relevant evidence, including quotations.

FURTHER QUESTIONS

1 In the Epilogue, Prospero speaks directly to the audience about the performance they have just watched. Explain how Shakespeare explores the themes of theatre, and spectacle in the Epilogue and at least two other extracts from the play.

2 Write about the significance of the island in *The Tempest*.

Consider:

● how the island is described in the play

● its effectiveness as a setting

3 In Act III Scene 1, Ferdinand has been made to carry wood for Prospero. Read from line 1 ('There be some sports are painful') to line 67 ('for your sake/Am I this patient log man'). Write about how Shakespeare presents Ferdinand in this extract and in the play as a whole.

LITERARY TERMS

allegorical	having a deeper meaning that can be interpreted by thinking about what objects and characters in the story symbolise
alliteration	where a sound is repeated at the beginning (or on the stressed syllables) of multiple words to create particular effects
allusion	an indirect reference to something, e.g. another text
antagonist	character in opposition to the protagonist or hero
aside	where characters speak freely as if other characters cannot hear them
assonance	when two or more words close to one another repeat the same vowel sound, e.g. 'the billows spoke'
blank verse	unrhymed verse in iambic pentameter
compound word	two words linked with a hyphen to create a new meaning, e.g. 'sea-swallowed'
epic poem	long narrative poem, written in elevated style about the exploits of superhuman heroes
epilogue	a final comment by the author at the end of a piece of writing
extended metaphor	a metaphor that is introduced and then developed throughout all or part of a work
feminine ending	a line of verse that ends with an unstressed syllable
foreshadow	when an author hints at what is to come
genre	a type or style of literature, for example, comedy or tragedy
iambic pentameter	a metre where each line is made up of five iambs. An iamb is an unstressed syllable followed by a stressed syllable
imagery	creating a word picture; common forms are metaphors and similes
irony	saying one thing while meaning another, often through understatement, concealment or indirect statement. Dramatic irony is when the audience or reader is aware of something the character is not
juxtaposition	two ideas, events or scenes placed close to each other with contrasting effect
masque	a form of courtly entertainment that included dialogue, dancing and music
metaphor	a figure of speech in which something, someone or an action is described as something else in order to imply a resemblance
motif	an image, idea, or situation which recurs throughout the text
onomatopoeia	a word which imitates the sound of the thing it describes, e.g. 'roaring'
paradox	something that seems unlikely but which may really be real; a statement that contradicts itself
parody	an imitation of something that is deliberately poor in order to mock it
pastoral	portraying an idealised view of country life
personification	where human qualities are given to animals, objects or ideas
prose	written as ordinary language without the line breaks and metre of verse
protagonist	the central character of a story
proverb	a short well-known saying that states a commonly accepted truth or piece of advice
refrain	a phrase or verse that recurs, often at the end of a stanza of a poem or song

repetition	a literary device where a word or phrase is repeated for a particular effect
rhyming couplet	a pair of lines that rhyme, often used to mark the end of a scene
romance	a genre of fiction set in a distant time and place featuring unusual events and characters
sibilance	a kind of alliteration where words close to each other have or make a repeated 's' or 'sh' sound
simile	a figure of speech using 'like' or 'as' to make a comparison
symbolise	to use an image to mean or represent something else, often an idea or emotion
tetrameter	a line of four metrical feet
vernacular	everyday language, including slang
verse	written as lines of poetry with a regular metre as distinct from prose

CHECKPOINT ANSWERS

1 They are brothers.

2 He is wearing a gown or cloak that gives him magical powers.

3 Ferdinand's father is King Alonso, and Ferdinand believes Alonso has drowned in the storm.

4 Alonso does not believe him.

5 From Tunis, where they had attended a wedding.

6 Guard and protect him.

7 Stephano says he 'escaped upon a butt of sack' (cask of white wine) and Trinculo says he swam ashore 'like a duck'.

8 Create dams to make pools for fishing, fetch in firewood, scrape dirty plates and wash the dishes.

9 Her name.

10 A nail, a log, a stake, a knife.

11 Gonzalo because he asks 'why stand you/In this strange stare?'

12 She descends from the skies.

13 Ceres.

14 Suffer aches, cramps and pinches inflicted by Prospero's 'goblins'.

15 Bury it deep in the earth.

16 Clean and tidy his 'cell' ready for guests.

PROGRESS AND REVISION CHECK ANSWERS

PART TWO, pp. 8–36

SECTION ONE

1. Antonio.

2. Naples.

3. She remembers four or five women who looked after her.

4. Gonzalo's.

5. His cloak or gown, his staff and his book.

6. The mariners.

7. Ferdinand.

8. Sailing back to Naples.

9. Sycorax.

10. In a pine tree.

11. Being a traitor.

12. She is Alonso's daughter and Ferdinand's sister.

13. Kill his brother Alonso and take his crown.

14. Stephano is a butler and Trinculo is a jester.

15. Caliban and Trinculo.

16. Miranda.

17. A banquet.

18. 'Trumpery' (showy trinkets and clothes).

19. Chess.

20. The boatswain.

SECTION TWO

Task 1

- This scene is a dramatic opening and sets in motion the events of the rest of the play because the storm leads to Alonso and his companions abandoning ship and being washed up on the island.

- Even though it appears to be a naturally occurring storm, we learn in Act I Scene 2 that

Prospero instructed Ariel to create the storm. When the boatswain says, 'What cares these roarers for the name of king?', it is ironic because the sea-storm has been caused by the usurped Duke of Milan.

- We are introduced to some of the key characters from the play and learn about their natures. For example, Antonio and Sebastian are very aggressive towards the boatswain, calling him a 'whoreson insolent noise-maker!' and a 'bawling, blasphemous, incharitable dog'. This is consistent with their language and attitudes elsewhere.

- A theme of the scene is power and authority. On board the ship in these desperate conditions, there is a kind of role reversal as the boatswain issues orders to the noblemen: 'keep below'. This foreshadows the instances later in the play of characters challenging those in power.

Task 2

- The two men discuss the idea that Sebastian could challenge his brother Alonso's authority. Antonio tempts Sebastian with persuasive phrases such as 'My strong imagination sees a crown/Dropping upon thy head' and 'methinks I see it in thy face,/What thou shouldst be'.

- Antonio and Sebastian talk about who Alonso's heir will be. If Ferdinand is dead and Claribel overseas, then Sebastian is the next in line. Antonio is trying to convince Sebastian that he would be heir to his brother's crown.

- Antonio draws parallels with his own success in overthrowing his brother Prospero. Sebastian eventually decides to emulate Antonio – 'As thou got'st Milan,/ I'll come by Naples' – and overthrow his powerful brother.

- A parallel can also be drawn with Stephano, Trinculo and Caliban's plot against Prospero that we learn about in Act II Scene 2, Act III Scene 2 and Act IV Scene 1. Ariel interrupts this plot before any harm can be done, in the same way he does in the plot against Alonso.

PART THREE, pp. 39–52

SECTION ONE

1. The boatswain.

2. They are brothers.

3. Sycorax.

4. A teenager of fourteen or fifteen.

5. Gonzalo and Adrian.

6. Francisco.

7. Alonso.

8. Stephano.

9. Juno, Iris and Ceres.

10. Prospero.

SECTION TWO

- In Act I Scene 2, Caliban describes how he feels Prospero has treated him. The audience may feel sympathy listening to his account of how he welcomed Prospero to the island but then had the island taken from him: 'This island's mine …/Which thou tak'st from me'.

- However, Prospero and Miranda's account of Caliban's conduct is less sympathetic as they make a serious allegation when they claim he 'didst seek to violate/The honour of my child'.

- His appearance seems to make onlookers confused and uneasy, such as when Stephano and Trinculo repeatedly call him a 'mooncalf'. Prospero also comments on his 'disproportioned … shape' at the end of the play. Although Caliban's appearance can disturb and his language offend, Prospero had hoped that 'nurture' could have a positive effect on him.

- Caliban's language can also be very beautiful – 'in dreaming,/The clouds methought would open' – and his yearning for a better life and failure to achieve it are affecting and even tragic as they contrast with his demeaning treatment as a slave or as a freakish specimen: 'This is a strange thing as e'er I looked on'.

PART FOUR, pp. 54–63

SECTION ONE

1. Tunis is where Alonso's daughter was married to an African king.

2. Miranda.

3. Travellers.

4. Sebastian.

5. The middle of the night.

6. The masque.

7. Marriage.

8. It is uninhabited.

9. The seabed.

10. Prospero.

SECTION TWO

- Prospero's books symbolise the power of knowledge in the play. Prospero describes how much he prizes them and Gonzalo kindly reunites him with these treasured possessions.

- The power of Prospero's books is also indicated by the importance Caliban attaches to them in Act III Scene 2. At the end of the play, as Prospero turns away from magic and returns to his earthly responsibilities, Prospero vows to drown his book.

- There are a number of examples of characters being educated in the play with mixed consequences: Miranda thanks her father for being her schoolmaster while Caliban curses his teachers for teaching him to speak their language.

- Prospero seems to be saddened by what he sees as Caliban's unresponsiveness to the education he received and concludes in Act IV Scene 1 that he is 'a born devil, on whose nature/ Nurture can never stick' (lines 188–9).

PART FIVE, pp. 64–6

SECTION ONE

1 Act I Scene 1.

2 'Nothing of him that doth fade'.

3 Prospero.

4 Miranda's mother.

5 In Act IV Scene 1 to celebrate Miranda and Ferdinand's engagement.

6 Eleven.

7 'over-topping'.

8 'humming'.

9 'calf-like'.

10 Repetition.

SECTION TWO

- Shakespeare shows Ferdinand and Miranda's instant attraction to each other in references to what they perceive as each other's perfect qualities using religious language and imagery: 'A thing divine', 'goddess', 'There's nothing ill can dwell in such a temple'.

- At the beginning of Act III Scene 1, Ferdinand conveys his romantic feelings for Miranda in language that suggests he sees himself as a chivalrous knight performing brave feats for the lady he loves: 'The mistress which I serve quickens what's dead,/And makes my labours pleasures'.

- Ferdinand and Miranda's language in Act III Scene 1 conveys the sincerity and seriousness of their feelings for each other in its similarity to wedding vows, for example when Ferdinand says 'Here's my hand'.

- Prospero also comments on the romantic love he sees developing between the pair. Upon their engagement, he tells Ferdinand to be 'abstemious' until their wedding and before the masque comments that Miranda is his 'rich gift' to Ferdinand, which gives modern readers insights into social attitudes to marriage at that time.

MARK SCHEME

POINTS YOU COULD HAVE MADE

- Prospero explains to Miranda how Antonio usurped his dukedom. Shakespeare describes Antonio's skilful political tactics.
- Prospero understands the part he played in his own political downfall. Although he criticises his brother's ruthless behaviour, he also accepts he neglected the government of his people.
- In Act II Scene 1, Antonio convinces Sebastian to plot against his brother. He describes how much he enjoys having power over others.

- Shakespeare presents the scale of Antonio's ambition in Act II Scene 1 when he admits to wanting Alonso dead.
- In Act III Scene 2 Shakespeare parodies the workings of royal courts; Stephano has power over others, and Caliban tries to win his favour.
- At the end of the play, as Prospero prepares to return to Milan, Shakespeare contrasts his magical powers with his earthly ones. Prospero talks about removing his magic robes and objects and appearing before Alonso 'as I was sometime Milan'.

GENERAL SKILLS

Make a judgement about your level based on the points you made (above) and the skills you showed.

Level	Key elements	Writing skills	Tick your level
Very high	**Very well-structured answer which gives a rounded and convincing viewpoint.** You use very detailed analysis of the writer's methods and effects on the reader, using precise references which are fluently woven into what you say. You draw inferences, consider more than one perspective or angle, including the context where relevant, and make interpretations about the text as a whole.	You spell and punctuate with consistent accuracy, and use a very wide range of vocabulary and sentence structures to achieve effective control of meaning.	
Good to high	**A thoughtful, detailed response with well-chosen references.** At the top end, you address all aspects of the task in a clearly expressed way, and examine key aspects in detail. You are beginning to consider implications, explore alternative interpretations or ideas; at the top end, you do this fairly regularly and with some confidence.	You spell and punctuate with considerable accuracy, and use a good range of vocabulary and sentence structures to achieve general control of meaning.	
Mid	**A consistent response with clear understanding of the main ideas shown.** You use a range of references to support your ideas and your viewpoint is logical and easy to follow. Some evidence of commenting on writers' effects, though more needed.	You spell and punctuate with reasonable accuracy, and use a reasonable range of vocabulary and sentence structures.	
Lower	**Some relevant ideas but an inconsistent and rather simple response in places.** You show you have understood the task and you make some points to support what you say, but the evidence is not always well chosen. Your analysis is a bit basic and you do not comment in much detail on the writer's methods.	Your spelling and punctuation is inconsistent and your vocabulary and sentence structures are both limited. Some of these make your meaning unclear.	